KUESEL
ON
CLOSING
SALES

Harry N. Kuesel

PRENTICE-HALL, INC.

Kuesel **On**
Closing Sales

ENGLEWOOD CLIFFS, N.J.

Other books by the author:

HOW TO SELL AGAINST TOUGH COMPETITION
THE FINE ART OF CLOSING LIFE INSURANCE SALES
THE FINE ART OF FINDING LIFE INSURANCE BUYERS

Kuesel on Closing Sales, by Harry N. Kuesel

© 1965 by Prentice-Hall, Inc., Englewood Cliffs, N.J.

Library of Congress Catalog Card Number: 65–10530

Reward Edition . . . . . . September 1979

PRINTED IN THE UNITED STATES OF AMERICA

To my sons
Harry and Tom

The Scope of the Book

The purpose of this book is to strengthen your skills in the critical area of *Closing the Sale*.

The Art of Closing

Instead of satisfying the wants of a horde of over-eager prospects, today's salesman is faced with the necessity of seeking out people and persuading them to spend their money for his goods instead of the other fellow's. If today's buyer has more dollars to spend than before, he is also more discriminating in deciding where he will spend them. Consequently, the salesman must become more expert in:

Helping the Buyer Make the Right Decision

Most people simply cannot make buying decisions without assistance. Sandberg says, "There is no agony like that of indecision." A person who finds it difficult to decide is grateful when someone else assumes the responsibility for the decision and furnishes acceptable reasons for making it. Your job as a salesman is to help the prospect to make up his mind. He will appreciate your assistance, if only you will be good enough to supply it.

When to Close

Probably the most important thing to remember about closing is that it is *not* a separate procedure that follows after the other steps in the selling process have been completed.

Actually, closing starts at the very beginning of your approach. It is sparked by your attitude and appearance, by *what* you say and *how* you say it. It continues throughout the interview as you "button down" each successive point of agreement.

The close is well under way the first time you get your prospect to say "Yes," perhaps only by a nod of the head. As he keeps nodding agreement with what you are telling him, he finds it increasingly difficult not to continue. His actual decision comes about as part of a natural sequence, and he signifies his approval by permitting you to complete the order. You have helped him decide!

Don't Miss the Bus

The point of decision may arrive much sooner than you expect. Your prospect may have been half sold before you came in the door. Top salesmen agree that the most common mistake is not to close soon enough. Closing is not necessarily like the third act of a play. If you wait too long you may find that the curtain has been rung down and the audience has left the hall.

The salesman who waits for his prospect to make the first move may be doomed to disappointment and failure. Many people need to be prodded into making a decision instead of yielding to the temptation of "shopping around." Such buyers often end up by expressing their gratitude and appreciation to the salesman who helped them decide.

Satisfaction is the Test

Unsuccessful salesmen frequently reveal the reason for their failure by saying, "I'm not a high pressure salesman." They are actually more afraid to sell than the prospect is to buy. The blunt truth is—no pressure results in no sales.

No salesman need fear to be accused of high pressure if his sale meets one simple test: the satisfaction of the buyer. If the prospect is glad he bought, his approval of the salesman's role in the transaction is automatically implied.

The Steps in a Sale

The successful salesman is usually quite unaware of the various steps he covers in his closing of a sale. He has reduced them to a series of habits which experience has taught him will work.

The unsuccessful salesman is equally unaware of his ineffectual steps toward failure. His habit of doing the wrong things—or rather, of failing to do the right things—merely results in his continuing to miss the sales he should be closing.

Let us now examine the successive steps which one successful salesman follows from the beginning of his approach to the "happy ending" of the story: the completed sale. In the detailed account of Paul Strong's procedure in the following pages, marginal headings point out the various sales techniques Paul employs. A detailed discussion of each step of the sale, keyed to the marginal headings, begins on page 27.

It should be noted that not all of the 21 steps will necessarily occur in every sale, but a proper understanding of each step is essential to the development of expert skill in *Closing the Sale*.

Contents

The
Strong
Sale

Paul Strong, securities salesman for a leading investment firm, has just concluded a transaction with one of his best customers, the president of a large printing concern. He has known for some time that his client is a member of the board of directors of several other enterprises, including the bank in his suburban home town. This appears to be a propitious time to inquire about the possibility of getting some securities business at the bank.

1. Preparing the Ground for the Interview

Strong: Mr. Andrews, I expect to spend a few days next week calling on the banks in Sussex County. I know you have been a director of the Millville National Bank for some time. Whom would you suggest that I talk to there about investments for the bank? Mr. Hendricks, the president?

Andrews: Yes, it would be a good idea to talk to Jim Hendricks, of course. But I know what he will tell you. The man you will have to see is George Bullard, our Senior Director and Chairman of the Finance Committee. And you won't have to go all the way out to Millville to see him. He is the former head of the Bullard Paper Company and still maintains an office here in town. He spends most of his time handling investments for eight or ten estates for which he is executor and trustee, as well as for his own account and for our bank.

Paul learned that Andrews and Bullard frequently met on the morning train into town, and obtained Mr. Andrews' agreement that he would mention Paul Strong's desire to make his acquaintance. A few days later Paul telephoned Mr. Bullard's secretary and inquired about the best day and time for an appointment. She agreed to call him back, and a firm appointment was then set up for 10 o'clock Wednesday morning.

2. Getting Off on the Right Foot

Strong: Good morning, Mr. Bullard. My name is Paul Strong, repre senting Jones and Harris. I believe my good friend Frank

Andrews told you that I wished to meet you. He said you were
already well served in the investment field, but that there
would be no harm in our getting acquainted and possibly
exchanging a few ideas.

Bullard: That's right. I told Frank you'd probably be wasting your time,
because all of my dealings have been with one or two firms
where I have had very solid connections for many years. But
it's always a pleasure to meet another investment man, and
Frank seems to think you are a good one.

Strong: It's kind of him to say so. And he also told me that I would
find George Bullard a valuable man to know, whether or not
we ever did business together. He said that nobody would
think of venturing any investment decision for the Millville
National Bank without first obtaining your approval.

3. Building Personal Prestige

Bullard: How long have you been with Jones and Harris, Mr. Strong?
I've heard of the firm, of course, but I don't know very much
about them.

Strong: They've been in business for over 70 years. I went with them
directly after my graduation from Harvard Business School.
I spent several years in their statistical department before they
assigned me to call on their institutional accounts. I've had
the privilege of serving three or four leading insurance companies and a number of investment trusts; I also serve a
growing body of personal clients, among whom I've been
happy to include Mr. Andrews. He seems to feel that Jones
and Harris have done very well for him.

4. Sales Tools and Equipment

Strong: I'd like to tell you briefly how our firm operates. This booklet
will give you a general idea of the wide scope of our services.
In addition to holding memberships on the leading exchanges,
we maintain positions in a variety of top-grade securities, including public utility, industrial and railroad bonds and preferred stocks. We also have a special department dealing in

United States Government bonds and certificates. Here is a copy of our current portfolio of public utilities. I understand you handle a number of trust accounts for various estates. What type of securities have you been favoring?

5. Qualify the Prospect—Let Him Talk

Bullard: I usually confine myself to AAA and AA bonds, mostly utilities and high-grade industrials. Occasionally I'll venture into some field where I have a special interest, such as the paper and pulp business, where I spent most of my active business career. One of my estates was heavily committed in bank and insurance stocks, because the testator built his career in that field. But I'm gradually switching those into other securities to get a better yield with less market fluctuation. By the way, do you know anything about annuities, Mr. Strong? I have an 81-year-old cousin who needs a better income than the five per cent return she's receiving on her securities. She has no dependents, so there's no need to keep all her principal intact.

6. The Salesman's Attitude

Strong: An annuity would seem to be the perfect solution for her problem. At her age the return might run as high as 10 to 15 per cent, depending on the type of contract you selected. My friend John Ellis, treasurer of the Equipolitan Life, would be glad to give you the accurate figures. I sometimes recommend annuities to my clients when they want to provide a life income for elderly dependents.

7. Sincerity and Conviction

Bullard: By doing that you would seem to be depriving yourself of some securities sales.

Strong: On the contrary, these people have usually become my staunchest friends and clients. They seem to feel they can trust me because I don't allow self-interest to influence my recommendations. I've always felt that we in the investment business have a special responsibility toward people who know less about the subject than we do.

8. Close Early and Often

Strong: Incidentally, Mr. Bullard, you mentioned some bank stocks you were liquidating. I believe I could be of some service to you there. One of my investment trust clients is building up its bank stock portfolio. Do you happen to have any Chase Manhattan Stock? (*First attempt to close.*)

Bullard: No, these are all midwestern banks and insurance companies, and my regular broker is taking care of them for me.

9. Always Talk About "You"

Strong: By the way, Mr. Bullard, how did you get in the paper business? You must have seen a lot of changes in the industry in your time.

Bullard: Well, our family was in the paper and pulp business in northern New England long before I was born. Over the years, however, most of our mills have been taken over by the big water power companies and lumbering interests. We still own a subsidiary paper manufacturing company in Holyoke, which is run by my nephew although I still retain a seat on the board.

Strong: Do you have any Canadian investments, like Shawinigan Water & Power, or Bell Telephone of Canada?

Bullard: No, but I've bought American Telephone bonds and debentures for most of my accounts.

10. Make It Hard to Get—Easy to Buy

Strong: I understand there's a new issue of Southwestern Bell Telephone bonds coming out in a few weeks. It will probably be oversubscribed. There never seem to be enough of those to go around. But I'd be glad to put you down for a limited amount, to supplement what you pick up through your regular channels. (*Second attempt to close.*)

11. Start the Order Blank

Bullard: About what will they pay, do you suppose?

Strong: Well, they would have to be in line with current yields, probably around 4¼ per cent. Let me put you down for 25 bonds, subject to your confirmation when the price is made firm. (*Writes it down on pad.*) We may have to cut down the amount if the demand is as heavy as usual.

12. Objections—or Mere Excuses?

Bullard: I wouldn't want to deprive any of your regular customers, Mr. Strong. And Bill Norris always takes good care of me. Let's wait and see.

13. Supply Additional Reasons

Strong: Mr. Bullard, as I told you, I spent several years in the statistical and research department. Some of these estates you represent probably have some rather odd items when they first come under your direction. I remember a case where we were asked to track down nearly 50 different oil and gas stocks which were left in the estate of a lawyer whose practice had been in the petroleum industry. Many of them were cats and dogs, but we did uncover a market for quite a number that the family had considered worthless. Do you ever have that sort of a problem?

Bullard: Well, I had a cousin, Hal Turner, who was a mechanical engineer. He left his family high and dry except for a small plant in Ohio which manufactures a new-fangled engine, some new development of the jet engine principle. Hal thought it would revolutionize both the automobile and aviation industries. His son Walter is still trying to find somebody to finance it.

14. Enthusiasm

Strong: That's very often the case. Almost every one of our great inventors—Edison, Ford, Kettering—had to find somebody with money enough and faith enough to help him launch his bright idea. But that's what has made this country great—people who can dream up new products and new methods, backed up by other people willing to risk their capital in supporting them. It's a great thrill to be a part of it all!

15. Motivation

Strong: Of course, this is just an off chance. But one of our clients in Texas is a leading producer of parts for the aviation and space industries. We've done several undercover researches for him among small motor manufacturers. I'd greatly appreciate your letting me talk to Walter Turner. It wouldn't be the first time we were fortunate enough to act as a catalyst to bring the right people together. Wouldn't it be wonderful if we could help you perform a real favor for that family in Ohio?

16. Closing on Implied Consent

Bullard: Well, I always had a special feeling for Hattie Turner. Her husband was forever spending all the money he earned on promoting his gadgets.

Strong: Let's keep this quiet for the present. But I'll put in a long distance call to my Texas friend tonight and find out when he's coming to New York. I'd like to have you meet him. He'll probably want to ask a few questions, which will give you an opportunity to size him up.

17. Closing on a Minor Point

Bullard: This is very kind of you, Mr. Strong. Of course, if anything tangible grows out of this, I'd want to reimburse you for your time and expense.

Strong: Well, let's see what happens first. I'll call you tomorrow and let you know how I've made out with our friend in Texas.

18. Take Command

Strong: (*Next morning on the telephone*) Good morning, Mr. Bullard. I spoke to our Texas friend, Tom Thatcher. He happens to be planning a trip to New York next Wednesday to meet another motor manufacturer. So I told him we had an Ohio engine producer coming to see us on Tuesday about a financial matter, and it might be very much in their mutual interest to get acquainted. He said he would be delighted. So will you please call your cousin, Walter Turner, and ask him whether he could arrive here Monday afternoon, so we could have a preliminary discussion? How about the three of us meeting for dinner?

Bullard: You certainly haven't lost any time, Mr. Strong. I spoke to Frank Andrews this morning and told him about our talk yesterday morning. He knows the Turner family too, and he assures me that anybody Paul Strong recommends in such a situation will prove to be reliable and trustworthy. Unless I call you to the contrary, Walter Turner and I will meet you at the Hilton around 6 on Monday evening.

Paul Strong's meeting with Messrs. Bullard and Turner on Monday, and with them and Mr. Thatcher on Tuesday, proved friendly and profitable to all concerned. Turner and Thatcher eventually combined their talents and resources in the organization of a new company. Paul Strong had the pleasure of delivering $25,000 of the new telephone bonds to Mr. Bullard, whose regular broker was obliged to limit him to $10,000 because of other commitments.

Two years later, Paul could count a total of 14 new accounts he had acquired through recommendations and introductions by George Bullard, who is now a steady and appreciative customer.

The
Strong
Sale

(Analysis)

1

PREPARING
THE GROUND
FOR THE INTERVIEW

There is no better way to open up a new acquaintance than through the introduction of a mutual friend. When you are preparing to call on a new prospect, it will be well to consider how you may obtain a personal introduction to him from someone whose good favor and confidence you now enjoy. This may be through a chance meeting at some business or social occasion, a telephone call or a letter of introduction from your sponsor. The degree of your acceptance at the initial contact will usually have an important bearing on your eventual success in effecting a sale.

Importance of Time and Place

Many sales are made possible by proper selection of the time and place for the interview, just as many others are lost through poor planning of these important details.

If you are calling at the prospect's office, your first consideration will be to win the cooperation of his secretary or receptionist. She knows the best way to fit you into her boss's busy schedule—also how to keep you out! Unless you can sell her on helping, you'll probably not have a chance to sell him.

A Well-Planned Approach

Hal Donovan sold club memberships to business executives. He knew that Hugh Patterson already belonged to two other good clubs, but he felt sure that the location and facilities he had to offer would appeal strongly to his prospect—if only he could get in to see him.

The first time he called the receptionist told him that Mr. Patterson was out of town. He asked if he might talk with his secretary, then added politely, "By the way, what is her name? Miss Hughes? Thank you."

Miss Hughes was out to lunch, so Hal left without stating his business.

The next time he called, he asked for Miss Hughes by name. He was told to wait, so he picked up a copy of the company's employee magazine. When Miss Hughes made her appearance, she returned his smile and asked pleasantly, "Did you want to see me?"

"Yes, Miss Hughes, my name is Donovan. I represent the Corinthian Club, and I wondered if you might tell me the best time to have a brief talk with Mr. Patterson."

Miss Hughes asked, "Could I tell Mr. Patterson what it's about?"

"Certainly. We would like to offer him a membership in our new luncheon club. His name was suggested by one of our members, Dr. Halliday."

Miss Hughes was impressed by Mr. Donovan's courtesy and frankness. Unlike so many other callers, he hadn't filled the air of the reception room with smoke, nor become impatient when asked to wait. She felt instinctively that Mr. Patterson would be willing, if not actually interested, to hear his story.

So she said, "I'll see what I can do for you. Mr. Patterson will return from his trip on Monday. He will be extremely busy for the next couple of days, but if you care to call me around 10 o'clock Thursday morning, perhaps I can tell you when he can give you a few minutes."

When Hal Donovan telephoned on Thursday, Miss Hughes told him, "Mr. Patterson is making very few appointments for this week, but if you could be here at 2:45 tomorrow afternoon, he will be glad to talk with you for a few minutes."

Hal Donovan's customary practice of treating the prospect's secretary with complete candor and courtesy, in contrast to the subterfuge and condescension too frequently displayed by the insincere type of salesman, paved the way to a successful sale.

CHOOSE THE RIGHT TIME

If you sell to physicians and dentists, make sure of their office hours in advance so as to avoid wasting time. Lawyers are usually free after court adjourns in the afternoon, stockbrokers after the market closes. Teachers and professors can sometimes be seen between classes to arrange for an interview at a more convenient time. Saturday mornings are the worst time for calling on retail merchants, but the best for seeing office workers while relaxing at home.

NIGHT OR DAY

George Donaldson, sales manager of an investment firm, was complimenting one of his junior salesmen on a nice sale he had closed the night before.

"If I recall correctly, Dave, this is the third evening sale you've reported this week. That's very commendable. Some of our other men might make more of these night calls you find so profitable. But tell me, don't you close any of your cases during the day?"

Dave replied somewhat apologetically, "I seem to have better luck at night. I find that when I give my prospects a choice between seeing me during the day or in the evening, they usually prefer to make it after hours. So why buck them?"

Mr. Donaldson agreed that many of his own early sales had been made at night. "But my wife wondered whether it was really necessary. She reminded me that we made most of our own purchases during the daytime. Then I got sick, chiefly from overwork, and the doctor gave me strict orders to cut out the night work."

The manager continued, "What really cured me was a substantial sale to one of my neighbors. Pete Larsen was a traveling salesman who spent eight or nine months a year away from his family. When I suggested we might get together some evening to discuss his investment program, he asked, 'Why not come to my office Thursday morning? This is our slack season. It will be quiet and the children won't be interrupting us.' In addition to closing a fine sale to Pete, I met his boss and two other salesmen, all good prospects, which would not have happened at his home."

One salesman, who used to find himself making too many of his appointments for the evening, now uses a telephone approach in which he says to the prospect, "Most of my appointments are during the day. May I see you tomorrow morning or some afternoon this week?" If it develops that a daytime appointment cannot be arranged, the prospect appreciates the salesman's going out of his way to see him in the evening.

Using the Telephone

If properly employed, the telephone can be an excellent aid in establishing your first contact. There are right and wrong ways, however, to do this. It will pay you to observe and study the methods used by more experienced men.

Don Edwards, for instance, had been so uniformly unsuccessful in his efforts to make appointments on the telephone that he no longer tried, but instead took a chance on finding his prospects available when he called in person.

One day he learned that Jim Gardner, his company's top salesman in another city, was coming to pay him a visit. When he arrived, Don lost no time in asking him, "Tell me, Jim, how do you manage to see so many people every day? I understand you never call on anybody without an appointment. Frankly, I find the telephone my worst enemy. I wonder if you would be willing to call up a few of my prospects right now and use my name to set up an appointment for some time tomorrow or next day."

Jim chuckled, "I used to have the same trouble, until I learned how to do it right. I don't suppose the people in this town are very different from those in my area. Let's have some of your prospect cards and find out."

Jim looked over a half dozen of Don's cards and selected an architect named Williams. He dialed the number and greeted Mr. Williams' secretary in courteous tones, "Good afternoon. May I speak to Mr. Williams, please. This is Mr. Edwards calling."

The next voice was that of the prospect. Jim continued, "Good afternoon, Mr. Williams, my name is Edwards, Don Edwards of the Transamerica Trust. I'll only be a moment and I'll tell you why I called. . . ."

Continuing without interruption, but in a confident and courteous manner, Jim ended up by asking Mr. Williams whether 3 o'clock Tuesday or 10 o'clock Wednesday morning would be a good time for them to discuss the matter. "You say 4:30 tomorrow would be more convenient? That will be fine, Mr. Williams. See you then. And thank you!"

As Jim hung up, he found his friend Don looking at him in honest admiration. "Smooth as silk, my friend. I only hope I can measure up to the picture you gave my prospect when I see him tomorrow afternoon."

Jim assured him, "You will, don't worry. Now tell me, did you notice anything different from the way you usually handle such a situation?"

"Yes, right at the start," said Don. "I noticed that you didn't say *Hello,* but *Good afternoon*—first to the secretary and again to Mr. Williams. Any special reason for that?"

"I'm glad you noticed that. Sure, there's a reason. When I say *Good afternoon, Mr. Prospect,* he automatically replies *Good afternoon.* We have started out by being courteous to each other, and that makes it difficult for him to argue or become disagreeable when he learns I'm a salesman. I try to keep the whole conversation on the same comfortable level. And when he finally agrees to the appointment, I end up by saying *Thank you.* This helps to ensure a pleasant reception when I arrive for the interview."

Don remarked, "I can see you've put a lot of careful planning into that approach. Every word you used seemed to fit into a neat pattern. I don't suppose you've written out the whole script, have you?"

Jim smiled. "Yes, a few years ago I spent a whole week putting the right words on paper. Then I rehearsed it with my supervisor. He cautioned me to remember that our aim on the telephone is not to make a sale but merely to set up an appointment, *to make the prospect want to hear the story.* Courtesy helps, so does frankness, but most important is our confident assurance that he will benefit by granting the interview."

Jim took a folded paper from his pocket wallet. "Here it is. Frankly, I haven't looked at it for a year. Sometimes, after a long vacation, I get it out to make sure I'm singing the same tune as before."

As Don took the paper from him, he noticed certain words had been underlined for emphasis, vertical lines drawn to indicate pauses, other marks to denote inflections. And printed across the top, THE VOICE WITH THE SMILE WINS.

PRE-APPROACH LETTERS

Companies employing traveling representatives usually prepare the way for a new man in the territory by writing an introductory letter to merchants in advance of the first call. Many established salesmen follow the same procedure in order that customers will have the opportunity to review the stock on hand.

One salesman for a chemical firm never calls on a new prospect without sending a carefully prepared preapproach letter. He suggests three simple rules: 1. Keep it brief. 2. Mention a specific problem or service you propose to discuss. 3. Close by stating that you will telephone at a specified time to arrange for an interview. For instance:

Dear Mr. Manufacturer:

One of the new problems arising from the increased use of detergent cleaners is the prompt disposal of waste and residue.

A highly efficient method for meeting this important situation has recently been introduced and pretested by our company in a number of leading plants similar to your own.

I am planning to be in your area next week, and will telephone you around ten o'clock Tuesday morning to arrange for an interview when we can discuss the matter in detail.

> Very sincerely,
>
> John W. Salesman

When he telephones at the stated time, his prospect may raise certain questions before granting an interview, but the salesman is prepared to handle them by explaining, "The only way for you to determine whether we have something you will find useful is for the two of us to sit down and go over the problem together."

Frequently, if the prospect is not available at the time of the telephone call, he will have left word with his secretary or another employee—sometimes to make an appointment, otherwise, to indicate complete lack of interest, which saves the salesman an unnecessary trip.

Luncheon Appointments

Many salesmen close a large proportion of their sales at the luncheon table. If you find that your prospect is frequently interrupted by telephone calls or visitors, he may welcome your suggestion to have lunch with you. If he hesitates to put himself under obligation you can add, "Make it Dutch treat if you like. Both of us have to eat some time, so let's do it together where we won't be interrupted."

Experienced "luncheon closers" offer these recommendations:

1. Make the appointment for 1 o'clock instead of noon, to avoid having other people impatiently waiting to claim your table.
2. Select a restaurant where you can be assured of a quiet spot and will not be overheard or interrupted.

3. Don't try to sell while eating. Encourage your prospect to talk. Find out all you can about him, his family, where he went to school, how he got started in his business. Most people love to talk about themselves.

4. Instead of ordering dessert for yourself, have the waiter bring you a second cup of coffee and clear away the dishes so you can spread out your papers. If you have set the stage properly, you can frequently obtain a commitment before you leave.

5. Pick up the check if possible. This is easier if you have a credit card or charge account. If he insists on paying his share, suggest that he can do this next time you get together.

The same pattern can be followed in meeting a prospect for dinner in the evening, for breakfast when his family is away on vacation, or for a midmorning or afternoon coffee break.

Make It Important

In every case, make sure you will have sufficient time for an effective interview. Never suggest that "It will take only a few minutes," or "You will be under no obligation." Try to make the prospect feel that it is important for him to understand your proposition and its benefits for himself, his family or his business. A good salesman knows how to whet his prospect's appetite in advance.

What Would You Have Done?

John Underwood, a securities salesman, had been trying without success to obtain an appointment with Mr. George F. Dusenbury, the president of an important manufacturing company.

John's firm had acquired a block of unlisted mining stock from an estate in Illinois, and there was reason for believing that various members of a family named Dusenbury owned an interest in the property.

Each time John tried to reach Mr. Dusenbury by telephone he was told "He's at a board meeting," or "He will be tied up in committee for the rest of the day," or "He's too busy to make any new appointments this week."

Finally, John discussed his problem with one of his associates. "Fred, how would you go about getting an appointment with this man? He seems to be just about the busiest person in town!"

If you were in Fred's shoes, *What Would You Have Done?*

(*see* page 169)

2

GET OFF
ON THE
RIGHT FOOT

A great many sales are doomed at the start because the salesman got off on the wrong foot. Probably the surest way to do this is to be late for your appointment.

It is a good habit to arrive ten minutes ahead of time. Say to the receptionist, "I am a little early for my appointment with Mr. Taylor. Please tell him I'm here. I'll be glad to wait."

Nail Down the Appointment

To make sure your prospect expects you, it is wise when making an appointment to drop him a memo in the mail confirming the time and date. Many salesmen use a neatly printed card for this, "Confirming our appointment for _____ at _____ o'clock."

What if you are late? Should you apologize? Probably not, if it's only a few minutes. But if you are seriously detained for some unavoidable reason, try to have your secretary telephone for you: "Mr. Salesman asked me to call you, Mr. Taylor. He is on his way to your office, but was held up by a sudden emergency. He should be there by about 10:30." This will permit your prospect to shift his schedule, or, if this is not possible, to instruct his secretary to set up a new appointment for you.

A group of salesmen were reporting their experiences of the past week at a Monday morning meeting. One of the younger men said, "I seem to have trouble getting people to keep their appointments. Three times last week I arrived at the right time and place, only to have the prospect's secretary tell me that her boss was called away to a meeting, or he was out of town, or he just seemed to have forgotten about it. Does that ever happen to any of you?"

One of the older men spoke up. "That sometimes happens if we don't make sure that he writes it down. If I'm calling at his office and he agrees to an appointment for 10 o'clock next Tuesday. I point to his desk calendar so that he can jot it down just as I'm doing in my appointment book. If the appointment is being made by telephone, I tell him I'm marking it down on my appointment pad, and will he please mark it on his calendar too. Also, I like to make appointments for 10:15 or 3:20, instead of on the hour, to make him feel that I work on a tight schedule and won't be wasting his time."

Another man said, "If your prospect fails to keep an appointment he made with you, it must be that he wasn't sufficiently impressed with its importance. And so when something else came up, he found it convenient to 'forget about it.' It's the same as when a salesman says he just dropped in because he was in the neighborhood. If it isn't any more important than that to the salesman, it certainly can't be worth the prospect's time to listen to him."

Make Sure of the Name

Another way to start on the wrong foot is to mispronounce your prospect's name. Don't address Mr. Parkland as "Parker," or Mrs. Burnham as "Mrs. Burnside." If the name is spelled Taliaferro or Colquohn, a discreet telephone inquiry will enable you to learn the correct pronunciation and enter it on your record card.

The smart salesman realizes that his prospect is a busy man. Therefore, he tries to get as much advance information as possible. This eliminates needless questioning and waste of the prospect's time. It also helps to build confidence, because most people like to talk to a man who knows something about their business and its problems.

Don't Outsmart Yourself

John Harrison, Cleveland branch manager for a leading lumber company, had instructed his secretary not to disturb him for the next hour. "I've got to finish that article I promised to send Bill Jones before tomorrow's deadline."

Consequently, when Miss Swenson came in with an apologetic air and a card reading simply, Oliver S. McChesney, she was not surprised to have her boss ask sharply, "Who in thunder is he, and what does he want?"

"He says he spent some time with President Alston at the home office on Monday, and he was told to see you when he came to Cleveland. His train leaves in an hour, so he won't take up much time."

Mr. Harrison sighed, "I'll have to see him, I suppose, but why didn't he telephone first. All right, show him in."

As Mr. McChesney walked in, with his coat draped over his arm and a hearty smile on his face, he glanced at President Alston's photograph on the wall. "Good morning, Mr. Harrison, I represent Northwest Enterprises." Then he continued, with a nod at the picture, "I saw Leonard Alston the other day. He spoke very highly of you and suggested I make your acquaintance the next time I came to Cleveland."

John Harrison had known L.G. Alston for 20 years and was one of the few people in the company who knew that his full name was Lemuel Graham Alston—and that his intimate friends addressed him as "Gray" while others called him "L.G." and of course, nobody called him Leonard.

So poor Oliver McChesney clumsily exposed himself as one of those "phonies" who keep wondering why they get off on the wrong foot. All he had succeeded in doing was to supply John Harrison with a pat anecdote for his article on "Sincerity, the Salesman's Greatest Asset."

IMPORTANCE OF FIRST IMPRESSIONS

Sometimes a prospect will have received a negative impression about his caller before a word is spoken. Eccentricities of dress or manner may irritate him, subconsciously reminding him of people he dislikes. It seems unnecessary to warn against entering the office or home with a half-smoked cigar or pipe in your hand, even when calling on an old friend. There may be another person present who is easily offended by undue familiarity.

What do you do if your prospect offers you a cigarette? Most salesmen feel it is safer to decline, perhaps with an explanation that you are trying to cut down on your smoking.

A typewriter salesman remembers his embarrassment at the point of closing a sale for 30 machines to an important law firm. The purchasing partner, while waiting for his secretary to assemble the necessary information about the old machines to be traded, offered the young man a cigarette. Although he seldom smoked, the salesman thought it only courteous to accept. But a few minutes later, while bending over to copy the secretary's memorandum, he suddenly spilled a load of cigarette ashes all over the executive's desk which was piled high with letters and legal documents.

WAITING IN THE RECEPTION ROOM

If you arrive on time for an 11:15 appointment, it is not enough to announce yourself to the receptionist. If she returns from your prospect's office and tells you Mr. Brown is busy, make sure she has told him that you are there.

If she says Mr. Brown instructed her to ask you to wait five minutes, and if nothing happens for another ten minutes, it may not be amiss to look at your watch and suggest she tell Mr. Brown that you will be willing to come back at another time.

And now let's suppose Mr. Brown again sends out word that he will see you very shortly. However, when you are finally ushered in at 11:45, you hear him tell his secretary, "Please call Mr. Nelson and tell him I'll be a few minutes late for our luncheon appointment. I'll meet him in the hotel lobby at 12:05." What should you do?

It is only too obvious that he intends to get rid of you as quickly as possible. You will risk nothing by withholding your story until a more favorable time. But perhaps you can make him want to hear it by suggesting, "Since neither of us has the time today for a full explanation of how you might save a thousand dollars a year, let's try to get together on Thursday—for perhaps 45 minutes. Or would Friday afternoon be better?"

GOOD OPENINGS INSURE SUCCESSFUL CLOSINGS

What you say in the first five minutes, and especially *how you say it*, will frequently make a deeper impression than what you say and do later. Proper planning of your *opening* will often determine your chances for a successful *closing*.

One top salesman says, "The fellow who has difficulty in bringing his cases to a successful conclusion does not need instruction in closing techniques; usually he needs instruction in the beginning techniques."

This man makes it a rule to write out in advance the exact words he will use in the first 30 to 60 seconds. He says, "You may wonder why I suggest you do this. Well, when you discover how long it takes you to think of something to write down, you will realize how hard it will be to think of the right thing to say when you walk into the prospect's office. The time to do your thinking is when you have time to think. The prospect must be told at the start why he should listen to you at all. He must like you and your message so that he will say, 'Tell me more.' "

A good way to insure a favorable opening is to mail a letter or an attractive circular to the prospect in advance.

An office manager's curiosity was aroused by a folder he received in the mail, announcing the latest improvement in portable check protectors. Across the upper corner was a handwritten notation: "Mr. Wilson. I'll be glad to show you this when I see you on Thursday. Bob Sterling." Instead of throwing it away, the prospect kept the folder in his desk tray to await the salesman's call. When the salesman walked in and began opening up his carrier case, the office manager's interest was readily apparent and a successful interview was under way.

CONFIDENCE IS THE KEY

People buy only from persons in whom they have confidence. They will not buy from a salesman who leaves any doubt as to his desire and ability to serve them. But the man whose opening words and actions sincerely spell "I want to help you" will win their immediate acceptance and confidence.

The Parker family, for example, had just moved into a strange town. The moving van had scarcely departed when a friendly voice called from the back porch. It was a milk delivery man who evidently made it his business to greet new arrivals.

"Good morning, Mrs. Parker, welcome to Jonesboro," he said with a smile. "I just learned from the postman that you moved here from Smithtown. You will be needing milk for the children at lunch time. Here are two quarts with the compliments of the Highland Dairy. My name's Martin. I usually come this way around 6:30 in the morning. Your neighbor, Mrs. Carter, has been a customer of ours for five years. I hope you'll let me serve you too."

Mrs. Parker was delighted. She bought some butter, eggs and cream, and thanked her new milkman for his thoughtfulness in placing a covered box on the porch for his regular delivery.

Afterward, she couldn't help comparing this pleasant experience with her cold reception at the meat market, where a surly butcher filled her order and hustled her on her way so he could resume his discussion of yesterday's ball game with another clerk.

Remember the old maxim: "Business is sensitive. It goes only where it is invited, and stays only where it is well treated."

What Would You Have Done?

Lew Cochran, New York automobile salesman, had been introduced to Frank Gilman at a country club where both had been the guests of a mutual friend.

While driving back to town, Lew asked his host, "What kind of car does your friend Gilman drive?"

"None, so far as I know. He lives in an apartment in the city. Says he prefers to rent a car or call a cab. He used to have a home up in Westchester, but no more. I believe he still owns a summer place out on Long Island."

Two weeks later Mr. Gilman's secretary, Miss Jepson, brought him a card reading *Lewis J. Cochran, special representative, ABC Motors, Inc.* "He called while you were out. He'll be back this afternoon. He says he played golf with you and Mr. Hunter at Wykagyl recently."

"Oh my gosh," said Gilman. "Try to get rid of him if he calls again." But at that precise moment the telephone rang and the operator said, "Mr. Cochran is here to see you, Mr. Gilman."

Gilman grinned at his secretary: "Guess I'll have to talk to him. Can't afford to offend a pal of Jim Hunter's. Send him in."

A brief but cordial handshake was interrupted by another telephone call. Gilman apologized and lowered his voice as he answered it.

Well, if you were in Lew Cochran's shoes, *What Would You Have Done?*

(*see* page 170)

3

BUILDING
PERSONAL
PRESTIGE

People hesitate to buy from strangers. They prefer to deal with a person who has won the approval of others. When you and I need a doctor or a lawyer we usually go to someone who has been recommended to us or is known to have earned a reputation for integrity and ability.

The salesman who enjoys some measure of prestige has a decided advantage over the one who is not so well known. So the first task of the new salesman is to "get a reputation." Oddly enough, the newcomer in the community or the salesman taking over a new territory is usually more aware of this need than a man who has been assisting the regular salesman in that area and therefore assumes that he will automatically inherit his predecessor's good will.

REPUTATION MUST BE EARNED

Earl Harper had been a successful salesman for a leading investment firm for ten years. The time arrived when he finally accepted his father's urgent invitation to join the family's thriving manufacturing business in another state.

Having enjoyed the goodwill of many loyal clients, as well as

41

the genuine regard of his employer and associates, he prepared this "thank you letter" which he mailed to 50 of his best customers:

Dear Mr. Jones:

After ten years of happy association with the firm of Smith and Johnson, I have decided to enter upon a new career in another line of business.

Since it will not be possible to call on each of my friends and clients in person, I am taking this means of expressing my sincere appreciation for your confidence and loyalty during the years it has been my privilege to serve you.

My successor on your account, Mr. Charles Clarkson, will be calling on you soon, and I can assure you of his complete competence and desire to continue the pleasant relationship between our firm and your good self. May I bespeak for Mr. Clarkson the same generous acceptance and understanding I have enjoyed at your hands in the past months and years.

> *Very sincerely,*
>
> EARL HARPER

One of Earl's best and toughest customers replied:

Dear Mr. Harper:

We are indeed sorry to learn that we shall no longer have the benefit of your sound counsel which we have found so helpful during the years we have known you. We shall be glad to have Mr. Clarkson call to get acquainted, but he should understand that he will have to earn his own reputation as his predecessor has done—by good performance.

The situation was reversed in the case of a young traveling salesman making his first trip through a territory formerly covered by a surly old timer who had finally retired. The buyer for a large department store, to whom he presented his card, remarked sarcastically, "So Thompson Brothers have decided to send you out slumming. Pete Atwater always felt your line was too highclass for our cheap trade."

The young man replied with a disarming smile, "Please don't hold me accountable for Mr. Atwater's mistakes. I make plenty of my own." The buyer grinned in return, "That's fair enough. Let's hear your story."

You Must Sell Yourself

Whether you are a new man calling on an established account, or a more experienced salesman wooing a new prospect, your first job is to make the prospect like you personally.

Although judicious mention of your satisfied customers or a letter expressing appreciation for some service you have rendered may help to break the ice, such "third party recommendation" merely sets the stage for your performance to a new audience.

COMPLIMENT THE PROSPECT

Your first step in this direction might be a complimentary reference to the prospect's home or office accessories, or to something you know he has said or done: "That's an interesting picture you have over the mantle. Where did you find it?" or "I liked that article you wrote for Trade News last month. It was very much to the point."

Such a comment may be especially welcome when other people have failed to mention the matter. A well-known journalist received scores of critical letters when he wrote an editorial about salesmanship in which one of his comments was based on inaccurate information. But when on another occasion he wrote a series of articles for a national magazine in which he paid a sincere tribute to the thousands of salesmen who helped to make our country great, he received exactly two messages of thanks and appreciation.

One of America's greatest salesmen, Thomas J. Watson, Sr., late president of IBM, used to encourage his executives to write notes of congratulation, condolence or remembrance on their personal stationery. He called them "grace notes," a most fitting description—like the little notes that lend enrichment to the theme of a symphony. Such grace notes can also add enjoyment and prestige to your sales career.

MAKING FRIENDS AND INFLUENCING PEOPLE

Your constant objective should be to become the sort of salesman with whom people like to do business.

Little kindnesses and acts of thoughtfulness which most people forget to perform themselves can set you apart as a person worth knowing.

One man keeps a 10 h.p. outboard motor in his garage, which he uses for occasional fishing trips. Whenever he hears that one of his customers is going on vacation, he makes it available to him. "If he takes it, I have saved him some $20 or $30, and it doesn't cost me a nickel."

When Ralph Peterson finished his call at a factory where he had picked up his monthly order for shipping room supplies, he found it was raining hard. As he started to fetch his car from the covered parking area, he noticed the assistant buyer anxiously looking at the the darkening sky. Ralph called out, "Can I give you a lift, Mr. Morgan? Seems as though it won't be letting up for a while "

Mr. Morgan explained that because his wife had the car he had a problem getting home for lunch. "But I don't want to take you out of your way, Mr. Peterson." Ralph insisted on taking him home, saying that it was on the road to his next stop. Actually, it was a considerable distance from his own luncheon appointment. But when he explained the reason for his tardiness to the friend who was patiently waiting, it was easy for him to understand why "everybody likes Ralph."

COMMUNITY ACTIVITIES

Not long ago a veteran salesman was the guest of honor at a dinner in celebration of his 25th anniversary with the company he represents. The president of his company had written to a number of his friends and clients, suggesting that they might wish to send a message which could be included with others to be presented to Mr. Thompson on this occasion.

The response was literally overwhelming. Most of the letters and telegrams contained the usual expressions of good will and congratulations. But a great many people had clearly welcomed this opportunity to give utterance to their deeper feelings of sincere regard and esteem for their good friend and counselor.

After the toastmaster had read more than a dozen of these messages to the assembled guests, he remarked, "Most of us have been aware of Roy Thompson's deep and abiding interest in this community and its people. But I doubt that any of us has realized the number of channels through which his good influence has been at work. He is on the board of trustees of his church, and has served as head of the Community Chest. He has been president of the Rotary Club and vice president of the Chamber of Commerce.

"And yet I can say this from my own personal knowledge of Roy Thompson. He has never been a joiner, in the sense that he expected to get anything out of it. He simply has not found it possible to remain on the sidelines whenever an opportunity was offered to be of service to a good cause or to any person in need."

MAKE THE MEMORY LINGER ON

Many automobile salesmen have become cynical about the loyalty of old customers. One man says, "Salesmanship and service don't mean much any more. Most car buyers nowadays simply shop around until they find a dealer who is willing to give them $50 or maybe only $25 more for the old car in trade."

Fred Folsom, on the other hand, says, "Most of my business consists of repeat sales to old customers and people they send to me —and they often tell me they were offered a higher trade-in elsewhere. Back in 1949 I sold a highway engineer. Two years later he was transferred to another project 200 miles away. When he decided to get a new car in 1961, he drove all the way here to buy it from me. Knew my first name, too. They'll come back if you treat them right."

Fred says that his job isn't selling cars, but selling *satisfaction.* Every morning he looks over the previous day's repair shop orders in search of *his* customers. Then he calls and inquires if the repair work was done to the customer's satisfaction.

People remember Fred Folsom because he makes the memory of his helpful personality linger on.

Many salesmen use calendars, pocket diaries and various types of regular mailings to keep their customers' memory green. An advertising specialty salesman devised a red plastic combination calendar and calling card, and posted it on every available bulletin board in his territory. A prospect who wanted to contact him found he had mislaid the salesman's card. But his alert little daughter remembered seeing one on the bulletin board at the local laundry, and so her father was able to get in touch with him. The salesman had been remembered for his helpful ideas when he called some months before. His unique "reminder method" provided the means of bringing prospect and salesman together when the time was ripe.

Reputation for Knowing Your Business

It goes without saying that the men we have been discussing know their business thoroughly; moreover, they know how the products they sell can best benefit the customer.

A good reputation must be nurtured and vitalized by continuing service of the highest order, or it may be displaced by a competitor who has found a way of doing a better job for your customer.

In an article on "How To Sell Today," Philip H. Gustafson writes: [1]

The job of the salesman is changing. In an era when all forms of selling are on the rise, his role, far from declining, is becoming more important. No longer are persuasion, personality and product

---

[1] Philip H. Gustafson, "How To Sell Today," *Nation's Business,* October 1960.

emphasis the only keys to success. The salesman not only serves as a marketing counselor in a day when marketing-mindedness is a prime business asset, but takes on a much broader function. He advises his customer on new products, distribution problems and engineering. He becomes a business counselor.

HOW TO CREATE A FAVORABLE IMAGE

Although personal prestige and influence often gravitate to a man who makes no conscious effort to win popular approval, there is nothing reprehensible about the salesman who purposely plans to create or improve his image among people he hopes to serve. In fact, most men who have acquired a good reputation have done so merely by their faithful practice of the Golden Rule.

Harry K. Gutmann, C.L.U., top salesman for the Mutual Of New York, is a leading exponent of this philosophy. He puts it this way: [2]

> Selling is more than a confrontation of buyer and salesman. It is the creation of a climate of natural acceptance, the acquiring of a "nice guy" reputation. It is the proper mixing of knowledge and people.
> Knowledge is valuable to the salesman only if he communicates it to a potential buyer. And that knowledge should be well rounded and general, not confined to the product or service you sell. It is deadly to have a reputation of being able to talk about nothing but your business. An insurance salesman I know seldom gets a golf game with anyone he has played with before. The bespectacled bookworm rarely gets invited to the junior prom.
> Good selling is not being a cloying flatterer, a Yes Man to a potential buyer, a Republican among Republicans, a Democrat among Democrats, a conservative among conservatives, or a liberal among liberals. It is, in short, being a normal man among normal men, a man among men.
> It is not only ability shown. It is also thoughtfulness to a neighbor, jotting a note to the couple whose 20th anniversary was mentioned in the social column, or whose daughter was married, or whose son graduated from college "cum laude." It's offering to get baseball or theatre tickets, and sending a book to the boat.
> It's a matter of putting your best foot forward lightly, of displaying genuine human interest. But all of it doesn't mean a thing if you're not well versed in the product you're selling and the many uses to which it can be applied.
> Most people look for two qualities in those with whom they choose to do business: ability and integrity.

---

[2] Harry K. Gutmann, *Working at the Job of Life Insurance Selling.* Louisville, The Insurance Field Company, 1963, pp. 32–35.

What Would You Have Done?

George Evanson, a life insurance salesman in St. Louis, had been selling over a million dollars of life insurance annually for ten years. He liked to travel, and especially enjoyed his yearly trip to Europe to visit his mother.

Returning on the steamer in September, he frequently made new acquaintances with whom he eventually had the pleasure of doing business. Since many of these lived in and around New York, the time came when he decided to dig up his roots in the Mid-west and transfer his operation to New York City.

Only one thing made him hesitate. How would he go about rebuilding the fine structure of personal prestige he had acquired during his years in St. Louis?

If you were in George Evanson's shoes, *What Would You Have Done?*

(see page 171)

4

SALES
TOOLS
AND EQUIPMENT

No fisherman, golfer or yachtsman would start the day without carefully checking all his equipment. And no good salesman will venture into the presence of a prospect without first making sure that he has all his sales tools ready for action.

Most companies supply their salesmen with attractively printed and illustrated material, usually bound in a portfolio for easy handling. These have been carefully designed, not only to present factual information, but what is more important, to *persuade prospects to buy.*

Keep your portfolio fresh and clean. Don't allow it to become cluttered with torn clippings, soiled pages or obsolete material. Learn how to handle each item skillfully and without fumbling. Careful rehearsal will pay good dividends in gaining the attention and confidence of your prospects. Putting on a good show is as important for you as for the Broadway stage star, and frequently more profitable. A bungled demonstration is worse than none.

Be sure to have all necessary forms available instead of having to make another trip. Good salesmen are not too proud to carry a good-sized kit into the prospect's home or office. One top producer says, "I'd as soon walk into my prospect's office without my pants as without my sales kit. I wouldn't think much of a doctor who came to my home without his stethoscope, or who discovered he had run out of prescription forms."

SAMPLES AND PROPS

Select the appropriate samples for your sales presentation. Make sure each one is clean and fresh-looking. A neat sample case always helps to impress the customer. So does the salesman's skill in presenting it.

Some men like to defer the showing of samples until strong curiosity has been aroused in the mind of the buyer. Others prefer a full showing at the start, followed by detailed discussion of selected items. Some products lend themselves better to one method than the other.

Try to handle your samples with the same loving care displayed by a salesman of plumbing valves who wrapped his special chrome-plated samples in blue velvet cloth. He treated them as though they were precious metal—which, indeed, they were!

If props are to be used, they should be as simple as possible. The scaffolding must not hide the structure of the sale. A salesman of fibre board places a short length of the material between two chairs and stands on it to demonstrate its strength and resiliency. A salesman of fire-resistant fabric proves his claims by inviting the prospect to set a sample on fire with a match from a match book which he hands the prospect to keep. Whenever possible, try to get the customer into the act.

COMPANY ADVERTISING

If your product is sold directly to the consumer, your sales portfolio will probably include copies of the company's magazine or newspaper advertisements, helping to revive or reinforce the favorable impressions already implanted in the prospect's mind.

If the product is distributed through dealers, you should carry a separate portfolio of your company's advertising, one item on each page. Be prepared to answer questions as to media circulation and coverage, particularly for dealers who wish to know the circulation of national media in their territories.

Make sure you know the contents of all your company's sales literature, so you can include the salient points in your sales presentation. When you use the wording and illustrations which appeared in the magazine or

TV advertisement, your prospect will be subconsciously reminded of the favorable impressions he has already received. On the other hand, there are few experiences more embarrassing than to have a prospect ask a question about some statement in the company's advertising which you are unable to answer.

"Oh, Yes . . ."

Incredible as it seems, there are still a few salesmen who feel that their companies' advertising expenditures are a "high class waste of money."

They quote surveys which indicate that very few television viewers are able to identify their favorite programs with the products that are advertised. While admitting that magazine and newspaper advertising may lead the public to buy cars, gasoline and staple food products, they insist that sales of a specific brand are dependent on the efforts of the salesman, and that the money spent on advertising might be better applied to raising salaries or lowering prices.

A more perceptive view is that of an insurance salesman who says:

> Before my company began its advertising campaign, prospects used to say hesitatingly, "I never heard of your company." Nowadays, when I introduce myself and the firm I represent, the cordial reply often is, "Oh, Yes. Your company is the one that tells people how they can retire with an income some day!"

"Oh, yes." Two words that spell immediate recognition and acceptance. Words that mark the threshold of another friendly interview, perhaps another valued customer, sometimes a whole chain of happily satisfied buyers.

That is why smart salesmen mail reprints or tear sheets of their companies' ads before calling on prospects for the first time. The same material is used to keep half-sold prospects warmed up between calls or to maintain the good will of established customers. Each reprint helps the recipient to remember—"Oh, yes."

On the other hand, there are salesmen who just won't go to all that trouble. But when a company has laid down an advertising barrage to prepare the ground for the advance of its "foot soldiers," it would seem only fair and sensible for them to take the fullest advantage of that support.

Standard Sales Presentations

Some salesmen stubbornly insist on trying to improve on the standard material furnished by their companies. Sometimes they are like the Kentucky mountaineer drafted into the army who looked with jaundiced eye on the shooting equipment issued to him by Uncle Sam and compared it unfavorably with his own pet rifle back home.

A top sales executive made this comment about the salesman who objects to standard sales talks and to visual presentations that keep salesmen on the track: "Selling is like playing the piano. If you're going to play for fun it's all right to play by ear. But when you start to play for money you'd better learn to play by note."

No one salesman can possibly afford the time, thought and money that have gone into preparing the standard sales presentations used by today's top companies. The leading actor in the hit play on Broadway doesn't improvise or ad-lib his lines for each audience he faces but sticks to the script which the author has painstakingly written to express the right ideas, in the right sequence and in the right manner.

Follow the Script

A new salesman, Bill Brandon had mastered his company's sales presentations and rehearsed them enthusiastically with his wife. After establishing an outstanding record during his first year, Bill fell into an unaccountable slump. So his wife suggested they go over his sales talk together, as they once had.

"Why, this isn't anything like the story you used to tell," she exclaimed. "What happened to those fine illustrations you carried with you last year?"

When Bill explained that he had worked out a shorter version that he liked better, she asked him, "But what are those other men using, the fellows who are doing so much better than you this year? Have all of them discarded the portfolio we used to practice together?"

Bravely facing the facts, Bill discovered that his presentation had deteriorated into a cold recital of prices and comparative statistics instead of the *persuasive* sales story which had served him so well in the past.

Not long thereafter Bill was back on the profitable track from which he had strayed. By using tested sales tools in the right manner, instead of improvising his own ineffective material, he regained his former skills and returned to his successful sales performance.

Importance of Showmanship

Following the script does not mean that actors or salesmen performing the same work are reduced to mere automatons, all uttering the same words and going through the same motions. John Gielgud's *Hamlet* differs in many ways from John Barrymore's or Maurice Evans'. Each performer succeeds in captivating his audience by his personal interpretation of the role, which he has carefully rehearsed under competent direction.

The salesman must always remember that for his audience of one this is "the opening night" which demands his top performance if he is to persuade his prospect to identify himself as a happily satisfied user of the product.

When the actor-salesman grows stale in his performance, the reaction of the customer-audience is quickly apparent. The prospect becomes restless or impatient. He is no longer involved in the story.

Get Him into the Act

One of the dangers to avoid in preparing or delivering a sales presentation is to keep it from getting too "talky." Short bits of physical action will help hold the prospect's attention, especially if he is invited to participate. A good way to keep him interested is to hand him a sample or a pamphlet in which you direct his attention to a picture or diagram illustrating the point you are making.

Good automobile salesmen make plenty of demonstrations. They invite the prospect to hop in so he can see and feel for himself. Such features as power steering, power brakes, smooth acceleration and easy parking must be shown in action to be fully appreciated. There are any number of products which can be most effectively sold through a simple but dramatic demonstration in which the prospect is asked to participate.

If the product is new or unfamiliar to the prospect, it is important to deliver the presentation no faster than it can be absorbed and understood. One man says, "Anything that can be misunderstood *will be* misunderstood, so make sure he understands before you proceed to the next step."

The salesman of intangibles gets his prospect into the act by asking him for a piece of paper. If none is handy, he takes an advertising reprint from his pocket, turns it over, and proceeds to draw a graph or rough sketch to explain the successive steps in his presentation.

It pays to develop skill in "talking with a pencil," riveting the prospect's attention right down to the point where you start to fill out the order and finally hand him the pencil to approve it by adding his initials or signature.

Use All Available Information

The Standard Register Company of Dayton, Ohio, manufactures office and factory equipment serving a wide variety of businesses and institutions. At each of its branch offices the company maintains a set of loose leaf manuals, generously indexed and continually up-dated as new ideas, products, uses and consumer benefits are added or modified. Included are such titles as Sales Manual, Product Manual, Systems Manual, Inventory Control, Payrolls, and many others.

Nesbitt E. Cockburn, New York district manager, says, "Almost every time I step into the salesmen's section of the office I find a man with a pad and pencil copying some item from one of the manuals. Perhaps he has an appointment with a hospital committee and he is bringing himself up-to-date on installations we have recently made elsewhere. Or he may be refreshing his memory about inventory control before calling on a shoe store buyer, or preparing an analysis of product turnover for a supermarket executive. All of our men are encouraged to contribute their ideas and experiences for these manuals. They know that the information hasn't just been dreamed up by someone in an ivory tower, but comes straight from the horse's mouth."

Don't Overlook Any Bets

George Shelly, a retail druggist in his early forties, decided to take advantage of a lucrative opportunity to sell his business. Although financially able to retire, he soon tired of travel and other forms of recreation, so he took a job as salesman for one of the leading pharmaceutical houses.

During his sales training and at the regular weekly meetings, George was especially impressed with the wealth of statistical information presented to the salesmen, with which they could educate retailers and jobbers in ways to run their businesses more successfully.

Tactful inquiry among the other salesmen confirmed his suspicion that this information was rarely used. Also, he could not remember a time when representatives of other companies ever offered him such valuable suggestions when they called on him in his old business.

So he came to this conclusion: "These men are missing a big bet, and so are our competitors. Any man with sense enough to use this statistical information ought to clean up." Which is precisely what he proceeded to do himself.

What Would You Have Done?

Fred Bates was on the floor of the gas company showroom when a lady came in to inquire about replacing a coal burning furnace with gas heating equipment.

Mrs. Wilson explained that she and her husband had recently purchased a lovely home with every imaginable labor-saving gadget—except for one thing. It had a coal burning furnace with an automatic stoker, which the former owner insisted was more economical and efficient than any other type of heating.

"But now, after six months of dragging the weekly ash can out of the cellar," she said, "and the added nuisance of buying a special grade of pea coal from a dealer eight miles away, we have just about had it!"

Fred showed his prospect various types and sizes of gas furnaces and water heaters, but explained that it would be necessary to make a survey of the premises before attempting to make a cost estimate.

An appointment was made for the estimator to call. A few days later the Wilsons received from Mr. Bates an official quotation of the cost of the necessary equipment, together with an estimate of the gas consumption for twelve months of average weather.

Since Mrs. Wilson had seemed so enthusiastic about the gas furnace during her call at the showroom, and because Fred had been able to recommend a smaller furnace than anticipated before the actual survey, he confidently expected to receive the order. But after three weeks, and with the cold weather approaching, nothing had happened.

Fred called Mrs. Wilson on the telephone, "Did you get the estimate I mailed to you a few weeks ago?"

Mrs. Wilson said, "Yes, yours was the first one we received. But my husband has several friends in the oil burner business, and we have promised them an opportunity to tell us about their equipment. There's still one to be heard from. I'll call you when we decide."

If you were in Fred Bates' shoes, *What Would You Have Done?*

(*see* page 172)

5

QUALIFY
THE PROSPECT
. . . LET HIM TALK

A group of sales psychologists were asked, "What common weaknesses in salesmen have you observed?" The answer was, "One of the first weaknesses we have noticed is that salesmen talk too much. If salesmen would learn to ask questions instead of making statements they would find the going a lot easier. Too many salesmen think that they are working only when they are doing the talking."

TALKING VS. LISTENING

Benjamin Franklin's first precept for establishing good personal relationships was: "Virtue is obtained rather by the use of the ears than the tongue . . . Put on the humble inquirer."

In other words, get your prospect to talk. Ask questions. Find out what interests him. Don't assume that the features you like best about your product are the ones that will interest him the most. Some automobile buyers look for class appeal, others look at the motor. One wants a big car, another a compact. This man's wife wants easy parking, the next asks about the service department.

One successful salesman says, "If the question method was good enough for Socrates and Ben Franklin, it's good enough for me. I ask questions. They give me an accurate picture of what goes on in this man's mind and heart."

TAKING THE PROSPECT'S TEMPERATURE

Mr. and Mrs. Leyendecker were in the market for a new automobile. Their trusty old car was beginning to show its age, and since Packards were no longer being manufactured, they were forced to consider some other make.

Helen said, "I hate to walk into a showroom and have some high pressure salesman try to talk me into a decision before we have a chance to look around. John, why don't you stop in at some of those places along the Boulevard and pick up some circulars we can look over together. If anybody tries to sell you, tell them you want to talk it over with your wife."

Mr. Leyendecker had much less trouble than he anticipated. Nobody was in sight when he walked into the first showroom. And after a cursory glance at the collection of chromium-decorated vehicles on the floor, he left without being observed.

At his next stop he again found himself the center of inattention. The blare of a radio from a private office revealed two salesmen so engrossed in a football broadcast that neither of them noticed the visitor until he was halfway out the door. One of them called to him, "Anything I can do for you, sir?" But Mr. Leyendecker waved a circular he had picked from the wall rack and smiled back, "No, thanks, this is all I need."

Two more visits left Mr. Leyendecker wondering just how he would go about getting the information he needed and wanted before attempting the selection of a new car.

He was actually relieved when he strolled into the next showroom where he was greeted with a pleasant "Good'morning" by a polite young gentleman who was closing the trunk of one of the models on display.

"Is this a Town Sedan?" asked Mr. Leyendecker, remembering what the dealer had called his beloved Packard six years ago.

"No, this two-door model is our Club Sedan. This happens to be the business model, very popular as an extra car for salesmen. We also have it in a deluxe model with a more elaborate interior. Do you use your car for business or pleasure?"

"Rarely for business, mostly for local shopping. And we take frequent trips to visit our family up in New England."

"Does your wife drive the car a lot?"

"Yes, probably more than I do, taking the children to school and calling for me at the station and so on."

"Then you might prefer that four-door model over there, so the children can get in and out easily. We have developed a new safety lock which can't be opened accidentally . . . Incidentally, we have shortened the wheelbase a little this year, and with power steering your wife will find it much easier to park. What kind of car are you driving now, Mr. . . . ?"

"Leyendecker is the name. We have a Packard Town Sedan. We've driven it over 90,000 miles and we hate to part with it, but up-keep is becoming a problem. How's your car on gas consumption?"

"That depends on the type of driving you do. On long trips some of our people report as much as 18 miles per gallon using regular gas. Of course, around town with a lot of stop-and-go driving, it's a different story . . . by the way, do you favor a high speed motor?"

"No, I'm not interested in a lot of extra horse power that merely uses up a lot of fuel. Just a good family car is what I'm looking for."

The discussion was interrupted by a telephone call for Mr. Jackson. He told Mr. Leyendecker, "Just look around, I'll be back in a moment."

The courteous manner of a salesman who took the time and trouble to inquire into the prospect's needs and desires was in sharp contrast to Mr. Leyendecker's earlier misgivings and frustrations. He began to concentrate his thinking on how much he might get in trade for his old car.

Having finished his telephone conversation, Jackson took a quick look at the directory and learned that G. E. Leyendecker lived at 22 Lockwood Road. When he returned to the floor his prospect pointed to a sports model and asked, "What do you call that color?"

"That's an Imperial Blue. Do you like it? I happen to have a four-door sedan in that color right around the corner. It belongs to one of our salesmen. Let's drive it up to your house and show it to Mrs. Leyendecker. We can bring her back here to select another color if she prefers."

"Good idea, Mr. Jackson. Let's go."

The very satisfactory sale which followed had been made pos-sible by the salesman's skillful use of "temperature-taking questions."

Use Short, Simple Questions

Until the prospect talks, the salesman has no way of knowing how far or near he is to closing. The question method, *if properly employed*, is the surest and quickest way to find out.

Salesman Jackson began by asking short, simple questions which no prospect could possibly object to: "Do you use your car for business?" and "Does your wife drive the car a lot?"

Questions of this type are seldom answered with a blunt *Yes* or *No* Usually the reply reveals more information than was asked for, indicating the directions of the prospect's thinking.

For instance, a life insurance salesman may ask, "What kind of insurance have you been buying?" One man replies, "Nothing but ordinary life for me. My Equitable agent says that's the only kind he buys for himself." Another answers, "My father introduced me to his Travelers agent who sold him nothing but 20 payment life. Now it's all paid up and he's sitting pretty." The next man declares, "I don't buy anything but term. I can handle my own investments better than the insurance company."

In any case, the sale has progressed much further by such an exchange of information than if the salesman kept right on doing all the talking.

WAIT FOR THE ANSWER

Some prospects are naturally uncommunicative. They are afraid of committing themselves until they have obtained all the information about the proposition under discussion. But the salesman needs to know what the silent prospect is thinking.

Perhaps Mr. Jones has walked into a music shop to look at radio and television sets. After being shown five or six different models he has given the salesman no indication of what is in his mind. Is it a matter of price? Or tonal quality? Cabinet workmanship?

Finally the salesman ventures a question: "Have you considered FM stereo?" Once more, silence.

In such a situation the salesman must not be embarrassed by the length of time the prospect takes to reply. He must remain silent while waiting for the answer.

The music store shopper may finally remark, "Which is the easiest to operate? This is for an invalid who knows nothing about music. Only baseball and other sports events."

The salesman picks up the cue with another question, "Would this be placed on a bedside table? Or would you prefer one of these remote control models which can be operated from across the room?"

Don't Interrupt

Once your prospect starts talking, try hard to keep from interrupting him. Only by listening to what is on his mind can you guide the discussion to the desired conclusion. And don't try to "talk down the prospect" if he interrupts your explanation. You are not trying to win an argument, but to reach a point of agreement. By allowing the prospect to talk himself out you will make him feel that you are fair-minded and willing to accept his judgment.

Don't Argue

Mr. Jenkins stopped at a garden supply center to look at power mowers. He showed the salesman an advertisement he had torn from a magazine. "Do you sell this make?" he asked.

"Yes, here is the exact model you see in the picture."

Mr. Jenkins asked the price. The salesman said $179.50.

"That's outrageous. My brother paid only $125 for a good mower two years ago. But of course, it isn't one of these fancy jobs where you have to pay for all the expensive magazine and television advertising. That's what's wrong with . . ."

The salesman remained silent while the prospect went on explaining his theories about the economic condition of the country. He turned instead to a group of other models and pushed one out to the center of the floor. "Here's a good mower that sells for $109.50," he said.

Mr. Jenkins stopped his tirade. "Well, that's more like it. Never heard of that make, though. How long has it been on the market?"

"It's made by a company that has been in the lawn mower business for over 60 years. Perhaps I should have explained that there are two types of power mowers. The one you saw in that ad happens to be a reel type. In addition, it is power propelled and it has a lot more parts than this one which is a rotary type."

"Which is the best?"

"That depends on several things. Those big machines you see mowing the grass on the golf course are the reel type. Many people prefer them, especially if they have a large expanse of lawn to cut, and some think they make a little less noise. But these rotary mowers do a first class job. We sell a great many of them, and we get very few complaints. How big a lawn do you have to take care of?"

Mr. Jenkins felt a bit sheepish for having popped off so quickly. Especially because the salesman had politely refrained from arguing while giving him the information he needed.

He ended up by buying a rotary type machine in a larger size for $129.75.

LISTENING BUILDS CONFIDENCE

One of the easiest ways to win the prospect's confidence is to get him to talk about the house or the automobile or the piano he now owns. But make sure of listening carefully the first time, avoiding the necessity of retracing your steps later on.

By listening to why he likes or dislikes his earlier purchase you not only learn what he wants, but also you impress him as a person whose recommendations will be designed to please him.

QUALIFY THE PROSPECT IN ADVANCE

Paul Price, a mutual fund salesman, had sent a letter enclosing a descriptive folder to one of his neighbors. All that he knew about John Jepson was that he lived in an attractive house and drove a new convertible.

When he telephoned one evening, Mrs. Jepson answered the call and explained that her husband had just left on a short errand but would return in 15 minutes. When the telephone rang again a half hour later, Mrs. Jepson interrupted her favorite television program and called to her husband who was downstairs trying out his new automatic drill, "Will you please answer the phone, it's probably that man who called while you were out."

Mr. Jepson wiped his hands and hurried upstairs to answer the call. A voice said, "Good evening, Mr. Jepson, this is Paul Price of Smith, Jones and Company. I sent you a letter the other day about our latest issue of mutual fund shares. . . ."

Mr. Jepson said nothing, but allowed the salesman to continue talking. Finally the voice stopped, paused for a few moments, then resumed, "Mr. Jepson, are you there? Did you hear what I said?"

Mr. Jepson's answer was brief and to the point. "Yes, I heard you. And I got your letter. And my wife answered your telephone call. And I stopped what I was doing to answer this call. All of which would have been completely unnecessary if you had taken the trouble to find out a little more about me. You see, I have been the sales manager for one of your competitors for the past six years."

By failing to qualify his prospect in advance, Paul Price had merely succeeded in making himself appear ridiculous, to say nothing of wasting his own and his prospect's time. John Jepson, on the other hand, was able to turn the incident to good account. At the next weekly meeting of his own sales staff, he described what happened and asked each man in turn to tell how he made his approach to a new prospect. Frank Hall, a former real estate salesman, made the following report:

PREQUALIFYING SAVES TIME

I learned the importance of prequalifying prospects in my old business. Our real estate office was in a good suburban neighborhood, and every weekend we would run a classified ad featuring a specific property we had for sale. It might mention 2-story brick and stucco, 3 bedrooms, 2 baths, expandable attic, double garage, reasonable terms, and so on.

The mistake I made, when it was my turn to interview a prospect who came to the office, was to assume he was interested in the house we advertised. Sometimes that was true, but just as often it was not.

I soon learned to start with a question, "May I help you?" The prospect might reply by asking whether we had any houses to offer on Prospect Hill. Or a young couple would ask about schools, another wanted something near the railroad station, and so on.

But this was only the beginning. I would write down what they told me, and then keep on asking them about other details: how many in the family, ages of the children, were they now living in an apartment or in a private house, in our town or elsewhere, and so on.

This would get them to telling me a lot of other things: Dad likes to work in the garden. Mother wants a modern kitchen. The kids want a rumpus room. Double garage is a must. And how about taxes?

Not until then would I get out my portfolio and begin to qualify them about how much they could afford to pay. "Here's an attractive place. The owner is asking $37,500." If this brought a negative nod, I would turn to another at a lower figure. Or they might simply ask how much ground it had, not mentioning any price. By this time I would be able to visualize the things that would interest them most. And when we finally stepped into my car to take a look at three specific properties which seemed to come nearest to their specifications, we would be saving a lot of time and trouble for both of us. Even if we didn't find the exact house they wanted that day, they appreciated my sincere desire to help them. And eventually, in most cases, we would do business.

Now, fellows, I grant that this business is a lot different in many respects. But I can trace practically every sale I make to the fact that I qualify my prospects so thoroughly in advance.

I learned about a chemistry professor from one of my satisfied customers, a dentist. It was his brother-in-law, whose wife had recently inherited a small estate. Conservative people, so I decided to eliminate anything speculative. The professor seemed favorably impressed when I didn't try to sell him the first thing that popped into my head, but took special care to select two or three seasoned issues that would provide a steady income to supplement his salary, and also offer a reasonable growth toward his future retirement.

To sum up the subject, the more questions you can get your prospect to answer, and the more sincerely you try to answer his questions in return, the nearer you are to closing a good sale.

What Would You Have Done?

Young Jim Jessup sold law books. His firm also published a weekly law journal, established nearly 60 years ago and highly regarded in its field.

Jim had been fairly successful in canvassing young lawyers for new subscriptions to the journal and in some cases had been able to interest them in a set of newly edited standard works for their library shelves.

After spending a morning working his way through the office building of the local bar association, Jim noticed the name of a well-known law firm on the doors of a tenth floor office. He telephoned his office to inquire whether Waldron and Pickering were subscribers or customers of his firm. A clerk told him they were not

The corridor bulletin board listed Jonathan R. Pickering at the same office number as the firm's listing, so Jim walked in and asked for Mr. Pickering.

The receptionist took Jim's card, picked up her telephone and said, "Mr. Pickering, a Mr. Jessup of the Roundtree Publishing Company would like to speak to you."

When Jim was ushered into Mr. Pickering's private office, he was greeted by a hearty middleaged gentleman who held out his hand and said, "Well, young man, what can I sell you?"

If you had been in Jim Jessup's shoes, *What Would You Have Done?*

(see page 173)

6

THE
SALESMAN'S
ATTITUDE

A television comic gave his definition of a salesman as "a chap with a smile on his face, a shine on his shoes, and a lousy territory."

Like the small town journalist who is convinced that he would have achieved greater appreciation and material success in the Big City, the mediocre salesman too often places the blame for his poor results on the limitations of his territory.

These arguments are refuted by the national reputations earned by such "small town newspaper men" as William Allen White of Emporia, Kansas, and Harry Golden of Charlotte, N.C., which are matched by hundreds of outstandingly successful salesmen who have confirmed the old adage "It isn't the size of the territory, but the size of the man in the territory."

It Pays to Be Positive

Dave Everett sold blankets for a Pennsylvania manufacturer in a semirural New England territory. After a modest beginning he gradually built up a loyal following of customers who learned that they could depend on him for reliable merchandise and close personal attention to their needs.

As Dave's business grew and prospered, he bought his family a nice house and a car and he felt he was "sitting pretty." Then, with no warning whatever, he found himself out of a job. The owners of his company, third-generation heirs of the original founder, suddenly decided to sell out to a competitor.

On Dave's final trip around the territory he tried to enlist the the cooperation of several friendly buyers in helping him make a new connection. None appeared optimistic, but one retailer in a small town suggested, "It might not do any harm to get in touch with Commonwealth Textiles. Haven't seen one of their men in a long time. Maybe they're not covering this part of the country, but it might be worth a try."

The following week Dave called on Mr. John Whittaker, sales manager of Commonwealth Textiles. His opening line was, "Mr. Whittaker, I understand you need a live representative up in New England."

"Who told you that?"

Dave answered, "I've been traveling that territory for six years, and one of my good Vermont customers says he hasn't seen anybody from your firm in all that time."

Mr. Whittaker smiled, "Maybe so. Our Boston man covers most of the bigger centers, largely by mail and telephone. The last time we offered that northern New England territory to one of our young men, he felt he was being banished to Siberia. He said nobody could make a living selling our line up there."

Dave burst out enthusiastically, "I've sold a pile of blankets in that part of the country. With your much bigger line of trade-marked merchandise to offer, that territory could be turned into a gold mine."

He got the job, chiefly due to his positive attitude about the territory.

Dave's first trip for Commonwealth, during a snowy week in November, took him into New Hampshire and Vermont. Merchants in St. Johnsbury, Bennington, Rutland and other ski centers greeted him warmly and responded to his enthusiastically helpful recommendations. While other salesmen continued to believe it was a "lousy territory," Dave carried his new line into large and small towns that hadn't seen a real live salesman in years.

According to last reports, Dave Everett's territory now stretches from northeastern Maine all the way to Buffalo, and he hasn't had such a good time or made so much money since he started selling ten years ago.

SELF-CONFIDENCE IS INFECTIOUS

The salesman's need for a positive mental attitude extends into every phase of his job; a feeling of self-confidence in his ability to serve his customer's best interest will automatically reflect itself in the trustful attitude of the buyer. A top salesman who is well known for his high degree of positive mental attitude says, "Before I see a prospect I reiterate to myself: (1) I have a good product, (2) My prospect needs it, (3) He will be much better off with it than he is now without it, and (4) If he's smart he will buy it."

A top sales executive was heard to say, "A man's success in selling is more dependent on his mental attitude than on his ability. There are more salesmen who fear they will lose the sale than there are others who are confident of winning out."

A new or inexperienced salesman is sometimes inclined to feel inferior in the presence of an important buyer. One man says he overcame his inferiority complex by imagining that he encountered the prospect on the beach in his bathing suit instead of sitting behind his desk in impressive surroundings. "The important thing to remember," he says, "is that I know a lot more about the subject of my call than he does, and that he will be grateful to me for telling him about it."

Attitude Toward Criticism and Complaints

Even the best of us may not be immune to an occasional slump, causing a temporary loss of self-confidence. When a star ball player like Mickey Mantle finds himself in a slump, he realizes the importance of regaining his winning touch by prompt analysis and correction of whatever he is doing wrong. Usually it isn't just one thing: it may be his stance, or his timing, the way he grips his bat or cocks his arm.

So what does he do? He asks his coach or an experienced associate to watch him in action to locate the difficulty. And when suggestions are offered, he accepts them in good grace instead of adopting the negative attitude so often displayed by less successful men.

The hardest man to help is the prima donna, the fellow who refuses to admit any mistake. By stubbornly resisting and resenting any criticism of his performance, he merely delays and may sometimes permanently block his own growth as a salesman.

The Art of Disagreement

Tom Campbell sold chemicals for an old, established firm in Philadelphia. When his local branch manager was transferred to an executive post at the home office, Tom half expected to be considered for the vacancy. True, his recent performance in the field was considerably below par, but a touch of the flu and some extensive dental work had provided convenient excuses for slowing down his pace.

So when the company appointed John Drayton, a younger man from a neighboring state, to take over the managership, Tom was inclined to sulk and find fault with the new setup.

Mr. Drayton took no notice of Tom's uncooperative attitude but concentrated his attention on the younger salesmen and on two or three new men he added to the staff. By the third month it was quite evident, even to Tom, that the new manager was making excellent headway. Most of the other men were enthusiastic about Drayton's new ideas and accepted his leadership without question.

One morning Tom surprised his manager by walking into his private office and asking, "Mr. Drayton, I wonder whether you'd be willing to make a few calls with me in the field. You've been so busy I've hesitated to bother you, but frankly I don't know what's the matter, so maybe you can help me."

Mr. Drayton reached for his hat. "I'd like nothing better. Let's start right away."

Tom suggested they make their first call on Jim Clark, purchasing agent for an important food processing company, an old customer of the house. "He telephoned the other day, asked me to stop in the next time I was in his neighborhood. Probably some petty complaint. He's always beefing about something."

Mr. Drayton watched the receptionist as she grimly took Tom's card and ushered him into Mr. Clark's private office. He decided to wait outside. The door was open, so the conversation was clearly audible.

Mr. Clark began, "I wondered when you were going to show up. I had some damaged containers to show you, but my secretary must have thrown them out when we held a committee meeting here yesterday afternoon."

Mr. Drayton heard Tom reply, almost belligerently, "You didn't say there was any special hurry when you called. Are you sure it wasn't the express company's fault?"

The door was closed at this point, so Drayton heard nothing more until Tom emerged fifteen minutes later. When they reached the street Tom told him, "Well, I got Clark to admit it was just barely possible that his receiving department was to blame. And when I reminded him that his stock of citric acid must be running low, he checked with the lab and gave me an order for five drums."

Drayton offered no immediate comment, but waited until they were seated in a nearby coffee shop. "I think I can pinpoint your chief trouble right now, Tom. It's true you won the argument with Mr. Clark, and he gave you an order besides, but next time you may not be so lucky. You seem to have developed a great skill for finding a point of disagreement."

"That's not so," said Tom.

"Well, you're disagreeing with me right now, aren't you?"

Drayton continued, "I watched and listened from the time you entered that reception room until you left Clark's office. From the way that receptionist greeted you it's evident you don't stand very high on her list of callers."

"What of it?" said Tom, "She's just a dumb clerk."

Drayton went on, "Since you were forewarned that Clark might have a complaint, you might have headed off his outbursts with some pleasant word of greeting, or an explanation that this was the first moment you had to see him. Instead, you let him start an argument —which you promptly continued."

Tom tried to interrupt, "Let me explain."

"I'm sorry, but you asked for this," said Drayton. "You've just confirmed all the impressions I've been getting these past three weeks. When we decided to change the time of our meetings from 4 P.M. to 9 A.M. each Monday, you were the only one to object. When the new report forms were introduced last week, you told everybody the old ones were much better. I'll bet when you got home last night you had an argument with your wife or complained about the children. You've just fallen into a chronic habit of disagreeing with everybody. . . . Think it over before you answer."

Tom didn't say a word for five minutes. Then he managed a sheepish grin and said, "It isn't easy to admit this, but I'm afraid you are dead right. I guess it's because of my Scotch blood! My mother used to find something wrong with my wife's cooking whenever she came to dinner. And last night Mary and I argued about bills for half the evening. I remember now that the first thing we were taught years ago in our sales training class was, 'Always find a point of agreement,' but it doesn't come naturally to some of us."

Mr. Drayton nodded "You have made a good beginning by agreeing with my diagnosis. It really isn't difficult to form the positive habit of *agreeing* with people—even if they say your product is no good, or the service is shabby, or they try to call you dishonest or untruthful. Just put on a smile and say to them, 'You must have a reason for thinking that. Maybe I'd feel the same way if it happened to me. Please tell me about it.' "

A month later Tom Campbell came into Mr. Drayton's office again. "I thought you'd like to know your medicine is working. Jim Clark invited me to lunch the other day. We have a golf date for next weekend. And when I brought home some flowers for Mary last night, she wanted to know what got into me. I told her you did!"

Proud to Be a Salesman

A good salesman loves to sell. He isn't ashamed of his calling, only of not calling. He never lets his mental attitude become clouded by the pessimism of the people he meets, whether customers, or prospects or other salesmen.

Like a good soldier, he maintains a positive mental attitude whenever he goes into action. He concentrates his thinking on ways in which his product or service can be of the greatest benefit to his prospect.

One happy veteran speaks about the *fun* he gets out of his daily work. He can't help chuckling at the close of a pleasant hour-long interview, remembering how the prospect began by remarking, "I can give you only a few minutes." And he smiles to himself when he recalls that a loyal customer who now refers to him as "my good friend" tried so hard to get rid of him the first time he came to call.

The value of a strong and positive mental attitude is demonstrated by the following comment of an insurance salesman who sells over a million dollars of life insurance every year:

> Before I telephone a prospect whose name I got from one of my clients, I know exactly what he's going to say—and so do you! In practically every instance he will say, "I'm loaded," or "I just bought a big policy in the ABC Company," or "You'd just be wasting your time, I had a survey done by my agent last month."
>
> We must never be disappointed or discouraged by such a response. I always come back with a chuckle, "Funny thing, but Jim MacDonald (the man who gave me his name) said the same thing the first time I spoke to him. But he has been kind enough to say that no other life insurance man ever opened his eyes to such substantial improvement in the insurance he already owned—and so we've become good friends. Would 10:30 tomorrow morning be a good time for me to see you? Or would 3 o'clock on Thursday be better?"

The Prospect Needs to Be Helped

A newspaper display ad carried the headline: *Which Salesman Will You Hire to Sell Your Product?* Below the heading were pictured two men, followed by the wording, "This man's prospects call him helpful, interesting, convincing. This man's call him tiresome, annoying, misleading."

The basic difference, of course, is that the successful salesman plays the role of the friendly adviser, the knowing authority who wants to help. But the role cannot be faked. It must never be put on for the mere purpose of making a sale. The surest way to kill a sale is to permit the impression that the transaction is more important to the salesman than to the buyer.

A famous character actor is considered by many of his fans to be a master of make-up because of the wide variety of roles he portrays on the stage and screen. Actually he employs very little make-up, nor will he allow anyone else to make him up. He explains, "I have to do it myself, in order to assume the deeper aspects of the character I am playing. If I feel it strongly enough, it creeps through and I don't need make-up."

ALWAYS EXPECT TO CLOSE

When Arnold Palmer lines up a 12-foot putt in an important golf match, he confidently *expects* to sink it. The successful salesman carries the same *expectant attitude* into every interview. Instead of going to *see* a prospect, he goes all out to *sell* him.

> The sales director for an electronics manufacturer heard by chance that a leading missile plant was in urgent need of an extra computer.
>
> Without any previous contact, he loaded an $80,000, 3000-lb. computer into a moving van and drove over to call on the president of the company. Explaining that he had heard of their pressing need for the new equipment, he asked where they wanted it installed.
>
> Two hours later the computer was in place and operating.

Another good trait of the real professional, whether on the golf course or in his sales capacity, is his attitude when things go wrong. When he muffs a sale he knows he should have closed, he remembers the advice of a leading golf instructor, "What happened isn't important, it's how you take it. The most important shot is always the next one. All champions keep right on expecting the next shot will be perfect."

ATTITUDE TOWARD COMPETITION

The difference between strong and weak salesmen is most often revealed by their attitude toward competition, particularly price competition. In nearly every sales organization there is at least one man whose constant fear is that the prospect will find out he can buy the article for less money elsewhere. He seems almost apologetic when he quotes his price —and then wonders why the buyer thinks it is too high.

The top salesman is not bothered at all when he learns that somebody else has offered the same or similar service at a little lower price. He says to himself, "There's one thing the competition lacks—that's *me*." He is proud of his price. And the salesman's "price pride" leads directly to the buyer's "pride of ownership."

A well known business author makes this observation:

> Have you ever noticed that the top salesman in any company, in any field, is extraordinarily *dedicated* to his proposition, his product, his service? He believes in it so thoroughly and so completely, and in the value his customers will receive in exchange for the money they pay for it, that they can't help believing it too.

Truly, most sales are closed, not because the buyer believes, but because the salesman believes.

What Would You Have Done?

Joe White and Sam Brown, home insulation salesmen, were attending a district sales meeting. The speaker was the company's advertising manager, reviewing the results for the previous year.

"One thing puzzles me. As you know we have been offering an attractively illustrated booklet to people who send in the coupons from our ads in the national magazines. We have been distributing these coupon leads to salesmen covering the respective territories, and in most cases that's the last we hear about them.

"Once in a while, however, we get a letter from one of you men saying you have made a good sale as the result of such a lead. On the other hand, some of you have said frankly that you consider it a waste of time to track down these leads and that you would like us to stop bothering you with them.

"I'd like to hear your honest opinions about this. Joe White, you're an old timer in this business. What's your reaction?"

Joe was one of the company's top salesmen, and his opinion was bound to be of interest to every man in the room.

He said, "I don't try to follow up any of these leads any more. The last one led me a merry chase, and when I finally located the address, it was an old people's home, where one of the residents likes to get free reading matter. Another time it was a high school student gathering information for a composition. I suppose next time it will be a salesman for one of our competitors, looking for the latest dope on our product. No thanks, I'd rather stick to my own customers and prospects."

Many other salesmen nodded their agreement with Joe. But then the advertising manager called on Sam Brown, one of the newest men on the staff. "Sam, you wrote me last month that you had closed six of the last ten coupon leads you received. Would you mind telling us how you handled them?" *What Do You Suppose Sam's Answer Was?*

(*see* page 174)

7

SINCERITY
AND
CONVICTION

If one could eavesdrop on the interviews of a truly successful salesman as he goes about his daily work, and then do the same with some clever charlatan who merely serves his own ends, the contrast in conviction might not be too readily apparent.

To be merely *convincing* requires simply the ability of expert persuasion. But the basic ingredient which must be included in every interview, if permanent sales are to result, is the unmistakable *sincerity* of the persuader.

A famous trial lawyer, shortly after winning a difficult case, happened to meet a member of the jury. When this juror spoke in glowing terms of the eloquence and persuasive powers of the opposing counsel, the lawyer inquired, "Why, then, did you decide in favor of my client?"

"Well, that was easy," replied the juryman. "All of us could see that you had right on your side."

The jury had been persuaded without being aware of the persuasion. Sincerity had made it easy for them to decide.

Sine Cera

The word "sincere" has an interesting origin. Sculptors and artisans in the days of ancient Rome took genuine pride in the perfection of the wares they offered for sale in the market place. Now and then they found themselves competing with unscrupulous imitators who covered up the imperfections of their product by filling in the blemishes or broken parts with wax.

This led to the adoption of a label which the leading artists then displayed with their articles of merchandise, reading "Sine Cera," meaning without wax. Hence our word, *sincere*; literally, without wax.

The Salesman Must Identify

A teacher of creative writing tells his students, "Just about the most important thing to a writer is what we call reader identification. If your reader is able to say 'That happened to me,' or 'I wish that would happen to me,' or 'What would I do in such a situation?' you have written a successful story."

The salesman's need for "customer identification" is exactly the same. Nothing is so convincing to the prospect as the feeling that the salesman would do precisely what he recommends if he were in the buyer's shoes.

That is why the amateur photographer believes the helpful salesman who doesn't try to take advantage of his ignorance, who persuades him to invest $40 less than he thought was necessary for a first-class camera. And that is why the sporting goods salesman who spends his vacations fishing in Maine or Canada is able to identify so readily with the buyer who seeks his advice about a fly rod or an outboard motor.

Put on Your Customer's Suit

Dick Andrews, young father of a growing family, had to spend his money carefully to meet a tight budget. He had not planned to buy a new suit or overcoat this season, but now he had been asked to serve as best man at the wedding of his closest friend.

It was eight years since he had worn that good old dress suit which had seen such frequent service during his college days. But the twelve pounds he had added to his sturdy frame since that time presented a serious problem.

When he called next day at the store where he usually bought his clothes, he found Bob Young, his regular salesman, busy with another customer. Bob asked him, "Can you wait about ten minutes while I take this gentleman to the fitting room? I'll be right with you." Dick noticed that the customer had evidently selected an expensive looking suit and topcoat, and hoped that Bob wouldn't try to suggest any fancy ideas.

Dick need not have worried. When he told Bob that he suddenly found it necessary to invest in a dress suit, the salesman asked, "Mr. Andrews, how many times a year do you wear dress clothes? Do you have to attend a lot of formal dinners and social functions? Some of my customers need to have several dress suits, while others wear them only once or twice a season."

When Dick explained the situation, Bob motioned him toward the elevator and said, "There's just a chance I can do something special for you." Stepping off at an upper floor, the salesman went on, "That man you saw with me a few minutes ago is a stockbroker who is in the chips. I sold him a dress suit last month for $185. It wasn't easy because he wanted to go to a custom tailor, but I convinced him we could fit him perfectly with the latest cut and styling."

He continued, "Mr. Andrews, I have about a dozen suits set aside up here for a few of my good customers who don't necessarily have to have the newest kind of notched lapel, or the latest variety of silk stripe down the side of the trousers. If we can fit you, it may mean a saving of enough money to help your wife buy that new dress she will be needing for the wedding."

As Bob Young filled out the sales slip 20 minutes later, Dick couldn't help remarking, "It's easy to see why your customers insist on waiting until you are able to take care of them, instead of letting some other salesman do it. You always put yourself in the buyer's shoes."

It is interesting to note that when your prospect senses that you have identified yourself with his situation, when he recognizes that you are looking at the question through his own eyes and seem to know how he feels about it, he automatically assumes that you know everything about the matter and proceeds to follow your lead.

He Learned It By Heart

An old-time salesman for a nationally known correspondence course attributes his phenomenal success to the fact that he was required to learn a standard sales presentation over 20 pages in length. And the story he tells makes it clear that he literally learned it "by heart."

Like a neophyte preparing for a career in the ministry, memorizing his hymns, prayers and texts from Holy Writ, I burned the midnight oil while mastering that wonderful sales talk about the wonderful course. I learned it word for word, line by line, and I believed it utterly.

The solid conviction I gained from that intensive study made me all but invincible when I faced a faltering prospect who tried to dodge or postpone my earnest efforts to persuade him that this was literally a cross road in his business and personal career.

I am sure that the many men I succeeded in enrolling, and who later became important members of the business and social community, were grateful for my dedicated labors in their behalf.

SEEING IS BELIEVING

Probably the most important section of an automobile dealer's operation is his used car department. No matter how many new cars he sells, he is headed for serious financial trouble unless he knows how to turn his trade-ins into cash.

Fred Folsom, whose record of repeat sales to old customers was mentioned in an earlier chapter, has been unusually successful in selling the "one owner used cars" he accepts in trade from his regular customers.

Since he knows when the car was originally purchased, and the driving habits of its former owner, he can say to a used car prospect, "You are looking at a pedigreed car. I can show you every repair order from the day it was first purchased." He asks the prospect to jot down the motor number, and then compare it with the original purchase order and repair slips. He may even suggest that the prospect call the original owner, but this is not usually necessary. There's no longer any room for doubt.

THE LOYALTY TEST

It seems axiomatic that a salesman must be in complete agreement with the policies of his employer if he is to act sincerely in presenting his message to prospective customers.

A top sales executive says, "Hand in hand with sincerity goes loyalty. If you must growl, condemn and continually find fault, then resign so you can do your damning from the outside. But as long as you are part of the organization, don't condemn it. If you don't believe in the policies and practices of your employer, how can you expect your prospects and customers to do so?"

John Morrison, a leading sales manager in the field of intangibles, has hired and trained hundreds of salesmen over the past 20 years.

During his interviews with prospective salesmen he tries to draw them out about their methods and attitudes toward the people they have been selling in the past. He does not care whether they have sold tangibles or intangibles, but rather how sincerely they have identified with their customers' needs and problems.

One morning his assistant asked him to interview a candidate who had answered a classified ad. His letter stated that he had sold mill supplies for a New England manufacturer. Previously he had spent four years representing an Ohio firm in the same line.

When Mr. Morrison asked the applicant why he was applying for a job in a line with which he had no familiarity whatever, he confidently declared, "A good salesman can sell anything. I doubled the sales in my old territory for Acme. And I earned $5,000 in extra bonuses during my last year with the Atlas people. Here are my commission statements for the past five years. You can see for yourself there isn't any doubt that I know how to sell. The product isn't too important. The test of a good salesman is simply whether he can bring in the orders!"

Mr. Morrison asked him why, in view of his successful record with his old firm, he wanted to make a change. He answered, "They are a cheap outfit. They promised me a larger territory but found an excuse to renege. When I recommended that we offer a special discount to certain customers where we were in hot competition, they turned me down. I know all about your company. It's the kind of outfit I would be proud to represent. And don't worry, I know how to sell."

Mr. Morrison concluded the interview. And the overconfident applicant never understood why he lost out.

Don't Oversell

Another pitfall to avoid is exaggeration. Somebody has defined an exaggeration as a truth that has lost its temper. Most people have had their eyes and ears so assaulted by the exaggerated claims of clamorous television and radio commercials that their automatic reaction to all such advertising is "I don't believe it."

Understatement, on the other hand, usually pays good dividends. Witness Ivory Soap's perennial claim, "99 and 44/100 per cent pure."

AIM FOR SELF-IMPROVEMENT

The English novelist, J. B. Priestley, was asked why several young writers who had studied with him had never matured in their art. His answer was, "The difference between us was not in ability, but in the fact that they merely *toyed* with the fascination of writing. I cared like blazes! It's the caring like blazes that counts."

How does a salesman learn to "care like blazes" about his job, about his product, and about how he can best serve his customers? A good way to start would seem to be to undertake a frank appraisal of his own personality and to follow a systematic program of self-improvement.

Benjamin Franklin, in his *Autobiography*, tells how he set up a list of a dozen desirable virtues, such as temperance, frugality, industry and sincerity. Then he concentrated his attention for a solid week on each of these in turn. He wrote, "Like him who, having a garden to weed, does not attempt to eradicate all the bad herbs at once, but works on one of the beds at a time, so I hoped I should have the encouraging pleasure of seeing the progress I made in virtue."

Although Franklin gradually gave up his experiment in personal perfection, he undoubtedly succeeded in establishing a set of good habits which contributed much to his illustrious career in public life.

WRITE IT DOWN

A successful salesman was asked to what he attributed his personal growth since he first entered business as a beginner fresh out of high school. He reached into his wallet for a set of cards which he called his "pocket pieces." He explained, "Most of us, when we read or hear a well-expressed or stimulating thought, say to ourselves, 'I must remember that,' and find a few days later that we have completely forgotten it. I formed the habit years ago of jotting down such items for my collection of pocket pieces. Here are a few of them:

> Failure is the chronic habitual evasion of doing those things we know we ought to do in order to be successful.
> An ounce of self-discipline is worth a ton of imposed discipline.
> Contentment eludes those who sefishly pursue it. It settles only on those who seek something good for someone else.

The best prescription for new business is to perform faithfully the old.

Being educated means to prefer the best, not only to the worst but to the second best.

When God wants to make an oak He takes a hundred years. But when He wants to make a squash He takes six months.

"Like Benjamin Franklin," he concluded, "I have derived a little pleasure from the hope that I have absorbed some of these bits of wisdom into my own personality."

What Would You Have Done?

Sid Saunders was a successful salesman of hospital supplies and medical equipment.

He had been trying for some time to interest Dr. Graham in replacing the sterilizing equipment and other office appurtenances he had acquired from his uncle whose practice he had taken over after his return from military service. But the doctor was a conservative type, inclined to "think things over" before making changes in his personal routine.

Like most good salesmen, Sid followed the trade papers and magazines and frequently called the attention of his prospects to some interesting item they might have missed. One day he spotted an article by a successful pediatrician who had acquired considerable good will in his community by establishing a free clinic in a Children's Home near his office.

Sid marked the magazine article and mailed it to Dr. Graham. A few days later, when he called at the doctor's office, he told him, "I thought you would be interested to know that Dr. Pelham, the author of that article, recently refurnished his office including some of our newest electronic equipment."

Dr. Graham expressed his appreciation for the article, but quickly added, "I've been following your advertising, and some day I'll probably want to look further into that equipment. But I simply can't afford it. At least not now. Maybe next spring. By that time we will know how true all this talk about a business recession really is. One of my patients, a banker, told me yesterday that he is advising all his clients to exercise extreme caution. The political picture is so uncertain. The stock market is entirely too optimistic, he says, and he expects to see a bear market before the winter is over."

In such a situation, and with such a prospect, *What Would You Have Done?*

(*see* page 176)

8

CLOSE
EARLY
AND OFTEN

A well known literary critic, reviewing a book for young children, wrote, "Very good, but too long in the middle." Many sales talks are like that. And you can understand why.

You have been taught or have developed your own interest-arousing approach, designed to make the prospect say, "Tell me more." You are doubtless familiar with a variety of closing methods to be used when the prospect indicates he is ready to buy. But how about that long "middle part?"

It is this middle part of the sales story, describing the product in detail and pointing out its wonderful benefits for the buyer, which frequently runs on and on until the prospect's interest fades, or some outside interruption prevents any effective attempt to close.

MEASURING THE MIDDLE PART

The right answer to the proper length of your sales story is similar to Mr. Lincoln's estimate of the proper length of a man's legs: "Long enough to reach the ground."

Let's assume you are a salesman of oil burners for residential heating. Some of your prospects may have lived in hotels or apartments and are therefore totally uninformed about the subject. Others may have acquired deep-seated prejudices which need to be cleared away. Still others may have blindly assumed that for some technical reason an oil burner could not possibly meet their special requirements.

For all of these prospects the "full treatment" may be necessary before a definite closing attempt will have much chance of success. But such prospects are by no means in the majority.

Much more common are situations such as the following ones. Since the last time your prospect talked to an oil-burner salesman, one of these things occurred:

He moved into a new home with an old heating plant.
His brother-in-law changed from coal burning to gas heating.
His neighbor proudly showed him his new oil burner.
He saw an attractive magazine ad and sent for a booklet.
His wife spent a weekend with a friend whose home was "warm as toast."

Any incident of this sort may have impelled him to think favorably about buying an oil burner, not necessarily to the point of asking a salesman to call, but definitely nudging his thinking so that he will listen more attentively the next time a good oil burner man crosses his path.

Give Him a Chance to Buy

Usually it won't be necessary to dot every "I" and cross every "T" before you ask your prospect to buy. He may be halfway sold before you come in the door. All you need to do is to finish the job.

You can never be sure of the right time to close unless you give your prospect a chance—and plenty of them—to decide.

There is a story of a young traveling salesman who wrote on his weekly report that he had called on 40 buyers. "But," he concluded, "after getting them up to the edge of the water I couldn't make them drink." Back came his manager's bristling reply, "Who in blazes ever told you that it is your job to make people drink? All you have to do is make them thirsty."

The Trial Close

You can't tell how thirsty your prospect is unless you test him. You may attempt a "trial close" two minutes after the interview begins—just as soon as you detect that he *wants* what you are offering.

Frequently he will reveal by something he says or does, or doesn't say or do, that he is "getting thirsty." He may ask a question, or ask you to repeat something: "Did I understand you to say? Exactly how much income would I get? Did you mention a portable model?"

A skillful closer will take advantage of such a "closing signal" by reaching for the order pad and saying, "I'm not sure that we have it in stock, but let me find out . . . how do you spell your name?"

The point to remember is that very few buyers will say right out that they are ready to buy. However, there is no law that compels them to listen to the whole sales talk.

Try, Try Again

New salesmen sometimes *fear* what will happen if an early closing attempt should fail. Experienced salesmen know there is nothing to fear. They merely resume the presentation and watch for a chance to close on the next point of agreement. One expert closer says:

> The beauty of the trial close is that it enables me to find out what the prospect is thinking. But I don't have to retreat if his reaction is unfavorable. I simply put him back in the sales oven and continue selling him on the benefits he will receive. If the trial close is successful, I simply start filling out the order.
>
> All closing methods are intended to make it easier for the prospect to buy than to refuse. The normal force of inertia makes it easier for him to do nothing than to do something. In a good close the buyer will find that he has to do something to keep from buying. If he does nothing he has bought.

"No" Is Normal

A successful old-timer says, "Very few prospects buy without saying 'No' at least once. Until a buyer has said 'No' six times it will pay you to keep on trying to sell him. In other words, five 'No's' plus one 'Yes' will equal 'Yes.'"

Another man says, "You will receive many 'No's.' But don't be discouraged. The prospect's 'No' is not 'Never.' And don't be afraid to fail. Courage is not the absence of fear, but the conquest of it. As Emerson said, 'The hero is no braver than other men. He is only brave a little longer.'"

The Swinging Pendulum

A well-known authority makes this statement about closing: "As the salesman presents his case, the prospect mentally swings from positive to negative to positive. That is why it pays to persist for the positive mental swing. 'Give a man at least six opportunities to buy' is merely another way of saying, 'Stay for the positive mental swing.'"

In the following illustration, arrows have been inserted at various points of the dialogue to indicate the prospect's alternating swings from negative (left) to positive (right).

When Mr. and Mrs. Johnson bought their suburban home they felt that it lacked only one important feature, a screened porch for outdoor dining. But with so many more immediate items to buy, they decided to wait until the following spring before doing anything about it.

While enjoying a weekend with friends in a neighboring town, Mr. Johnson remarked to his host, "I don't remember this attractive porch? Did you have it added since our last visit?" Mr. Clark said, "Yes, I'm glad you like it. It was done by a man in your town who specializes in this sort of thing. His name in Stratton. You might want to look him up some time."

Several weeks later Mr. Johnson was putting away his lawn mower when a pick-up truck stopped at his driveway. A young man stepped out and said, "My name's Stratton. I understand you're a friend of John Clark. He told me I might be hearing from you some time."

Mr. J.: "Oh, yes. You're the man who built his new porch. A very nice job. But we aren't doing anything of that sort. Maybe next year, if there aren't a lot of other expensive things to take care of."

(←—————————)

Stratton: "Well, I just thought I'd stop by and get acquainted. I'm doing a job two blocks west of here. Maybe you'd like to see it."

Mr. J.: "Is that so? Where is that?"

(—————————→)

Stratton: "On Beaver Road. The Stevens place."

Mr. J.: "Oh, yes. I noticed a lot of lumber piled up there yesterday. But that's a big job. We wouldn't spend a lot of money like that."

(←——————)

Stratton: "Most of my work is much simpler and less expensive. Do you mind if I look at your place for a moment? Mr. Clark says you have a very lovely home."

(By this time Mrs. Johnson has emerged from the rear entrance. Introductions are exchanged and the three of them proceed to the back of the house.)

Mr. J.: "Mr. Stratton says he's doing some alterations at that place we saw on Beaver Road."

Mrs. J.: "Well, we wouldn't be interested in anything so elaborate. We have a lot of other expenses right now. Maybe next spring. Not now."

(←——————)

(Mr. Stratton notes that the Johnsons have evidently examined the Beaver Road job rather closely and have been discussing the matter.)

Stratton: "Your place reminds me of a screened porch I did last year for the Youngs on School Street. You have the same sort of "L" between the side of your garage and the rear wall of the house. So there would be only two walls to build."

Mrs. J.: "What kind of material did they use for the roofing? I wouldn't want to have my kitchen darkened."

(——————→)

Stratton: "Do you plan to use the porch for meals?"
Mrs. Johnson nods.

(——————→)

Stratton: "With your kitchen directly adjoining the patio, I would certainly recommend a translucent material for the deck."

Mrs. J.: "I wouldn't want one of those blue or yellow roofs, which would spoil the appearance of our white colonial house."

(←——————)

Stratton: "You are absolutely right. Have you seen the new Noveltex material? It's very attractive in a snow-white effect that lets the light through without any glare."

Mrs. J.: "I saw something like that at one of the Flower Show exhibits recently. Is it expensive?"

(——————→)

Stratton: "Not a all. Let me bring you a sample. And I'll show you a copy of the plan we used for the Youngs' patio. With a few minor changes it would come close to fitting your situation."

Mrs. J.: "That would be nice. But please understand, Mr. Stratton, there would be no obligation. We'd want to get a few estimates before doing anything."

(←——————)

Stratton: "Of course. But you would save a bit of money if I could start right away instead of waiting until my busy season begins. I have five or six jobs booked in Roseville for the next three months. But with my crew working nearby at the Stevens place, we could do the two jobs almost simultaneously."

Mr. J.: "About how much do you think such a job would cost me?"

(———————→)

Stratton: "Probably less than you expect. Let me do some figuring tonight. I'll need to make some measurements now, and . . ."

Mrs. J.: "Howard, why don't you loan Mr. Stratton that copy of the architect's plan the agent gave us when we bought the house?"

(———————→)

(When Mr. Stratton returns the following afternoon, Mrs. Johnson invites him inside. He shows her the sketches he prepared and the samples of material he proposes to use.)

Mrs. J.: "I really don't see how we can justify spending the money right now."

(←———————)

Stratton: "You aren't really *spending* the money, Mrs. Johnson. You are making an *investment* in improving your home. It will add just that much to the re-sale value of your property. To say nothing of the pleasure and comfort you will derive from it meanwhile. . . . please tell Mr. Johnson I'll have the estimate ready for him on Thursday."

Mrs. Johnson nods her agreement, then asks, "When do you think you will be able to start work?"

(———————→)

ASK FOR THE ORDER

One of the most exasperating discoveries you can make is to learn that your close friend or neighbor has bought life insurance, or mutual funds, or an expensive hi-fi set from somebody else, simply because he didn't know you were in the business. But even if he knew it, he might not have bought it from you unless you asked him to.

One sales instructor likes to tell the story of the man who learned some years after his marriage that his wife had been a snake charmer in the circus. When he said to her, "I never knew you were a snake charmer," she replied, "Well, you never asked me."

AIM TO CLOSE AT ANY MOMENT

Selling is like a game. But not like all games. It isn't like golf, where you play against par, or aim to outscore your opponent. Nor is it like foot racing, where you try to outrun your competitor. You don't have to complete the full round of 18 holes, or run the full two mile distance. Your best chance of winning the sale may arrive at any moment.

It's somewhat like a tennis match. After you have served the ball, you don't say to yourself, "My next shot will be a short chop just over the net," or "I'll force him back to the baseline with a lob." It all depends on how your opponent returns the ball. Once in a while you can smash it quickly for a "kill." More often you will have to maneuver for position until you can try to "put the ball away." Even then he may surprise you by keeping the ball in play, so you keep pressing for that final winning shot.

Too many salesmen make the mistake of delaying their attempt to close until that elusive and completely imaginary "psychological moment" arrives. And so the prospect wriggles off the hook, to be caught by a more expert fisherman another day.

The Big One That Got Away

Few experiences are more disheartening to a salesman than to find that a sale which he felt he had honestly earned has been snatched from his hands by a competitor.

Dick Carpenter was a most conscientious life insurance salesman. When he returned Mr. Willoughby's policies after completing an elaborate audit, he outlined his recommendations for additional insurance to cover the family's basic needs.

Instead of trying for an immediate close, Dick let his prospect grab the ball away from him. "I can't tell you how much I appreciate what you have done for me," said Mr. Willoughby. "I'm not ready to buy all of that $75,000 of new life insurance this year. But I'm certainly going to take at least $25,000 before my age changes in October. I'm leaving for my vacation tomorrow and won't be back until Labor Day. Just call me around the middle of September and give me the address of your doctor so I can be examined. You have earned a good sale, and I promise you shall have it."

The salesman believed him. And probably the prospect meant exactly what he said at the time. But four separate attempts to reach Mr. Willoughby in September, in person or by telephone, proved completely fruitless.

Months later the two men met at a social function, and Mr. Willoughby sheepishly explained what had happened. "I've been avoiding you all this time because I found I had to break my promise to you. On our vacation up in Canada, my wife and I made the acquaintance of a wonderful couple. We played bridge and went sight-seeing together, and Jack improved my golf game by nearly ten strokes. I felt under such deep obligation to him for all his kindnesses that when he told me he was in the insurance business, I found myself buying $100,000 from him before I remembered what I had told you last summer."

Dick Carpenter has never forgotten that bitter lesson.

When your prospect admits he is under an obligation for the service you have rendered, when he is red hot and thirsty for the benefits you have convinced him he needs and wants, *close him then and there—* before he changes his mind, and before some other salesman walks off with the prize which you have so richly earned.

As William Shakespeare put it:

> *There is a tide in the affairs of men,*
> *Which, taken at the flood, leads on to fortune;*
> *We must take the current when it serves,*
> *Or lose our ventures.*

What Would You Have Done?

Mr. and Mrs. Hendricks walked into the Harmon Piano Company's showroom and looked around somewhat aimlessly.

A salesman advanced and inquired, "May I help you?"

"You don't seem to have any of those spinet models, do you? We don't have room in our apartment for a large piano like these."

John Kenyon replied, "Oh, yes, we have a wide assortment on the second floor. Just step into the elevator, please."

A half hour later, Mr. Kenyon returned to the main floor with his prospects, accompanied them to the door and bid them a pleasant goodbye.

Mr. Walker, manager of the salon, had been watching the scene quietly from his office in the rear of the store. "What happened, John?" he asked. "Do you think they'll come back?"

John shrugged his shoulders. "It's hard to say. They're shopping around. They wanted to look at a piano they saw advertised by a department store before they decide."

Mr. Walker asked, "But it seems likely that they *will buy* a piano somewhere, isn't that so?" John nodded. The manager continued, "And the man who gets the order will be the one who *asks them to buy.*"

John Kenyon colored. "You seem to imply that I didn't do my job. You didn't even hear the conversation, Mr. Walker. Let me ask you, *'What Would You Have Done?'*

(*see* page 178)

9

ALWAYS
TALK
ABOUT "YOU"

It has been said that "habits are either bobs or sinkers—they hold you up or pull you down." Good salesmen have learned to harness the power of good habits, just as poor salesmen have fallen victims, sometimes quite unwittingly, to the snare of bad selling habits.

One of the most valuable habits for a salesman is the use of the pronoun *you*, not only in your sales presentations but in letters, telephone conversations, and all other contacts with your customers.

At first, a conscious effort may be necessary to bring this about. An automobile salesman, about to mail a letter to the comptroller of a company where he had recently sold the vice president, was found guilty of "I-trouble." His manager, looking over the letter, found that it included such sentences as: "My client, Mr. Crosby, has told me about you . . . I am sure you will be interested. . . I would like to show you our new model. . ."

When the salesman was made aware of his over-use of the "perpendicular pronoun," he reworded his letter: "Your friend, John Crosby, has told me about your recent promotion . . . You have probably been giving some thought to a new car . . . You will want to see the exciting new Buick . . . Please let me know when and where I may show it to you, your associates and your family."

Successful salesmen sprinkle their presentations with such "you phrases" as:

> You will agree, I'm sure . . .
> You have found this to be true, haven't you? . . .
> You have noticed this, of course . . .
> You know from experience that . . .

A leading sales manager, long accustomed to "you-ing" his prospects and clients, has the habit of including a compliment and a smile in the letters and memoranda he takes the time to write to his associates or customers:

Good morning, John:

Your prompt reply to my inquiry is deeply appreciated. You have given me the exact information I needed.

I liked your helpful article in "Association News" last month. A lot of people will thank you for sharing your experience in handling such sticky situations.

Give my regards to your wife, and keep a few for yourself.

See you soon,

JOE

How Do You Like Your Boss?

Perhaps it is more important to ask "How does your boss like you?" Chances are the answer will depend on how well you have served him and how much he has come to rely on your recommendations.

No, we're not talking about your employer. We're talking about your Big Boss, every salesman's Boss—the customer.

In America every buyer has independent freedom of choice. Unlike people behind the Iron Curtain, whose choice of what and where to buy is dictated from above, the humblest American citizen can decide for himself whatever and wherever he may wish to buy.

Frank V. Bridge, general sales manager of General Motors' Pontiac Motor Division, told a meeting of the Sales Executives Club of New York:

We must never forget that our ultimate goal is customer satisfaction. I find that top-flight salesmen who are self-starters in their own right all possess <u>a fundamental appreciation of the value of a customer.</u> <u>Satisfied customers</u> are the hard core of their personal success.

"Boss" Kettering, who was as much a salesman as he was an inventor and engineer, used to tell us, "There are three profits in every retail sale—the manufacturer's, the dealer's and the customer's."

The first two profits are necessary and important, but the accomplishment of customer profit or satisfaction is the result devoutly sought by every mature, intelligent sales administrator and salesman.

The customer may not always be right—but he sure knows where he is going to spend his money.

"What Is Your Opinion?"

When Ambassador Dwight Morrow called on the president of Mexico for the first time, he merely passed the pancakes, praised the cooking, lit a cigar, and urged his host to *inform him* about Mexico. The ambassador had evidently heard that:

The most important word in the language is: *You.*
The two most important words are: *Thank you.*
The three most important words are: *If you please.*
The four most important are: *What is your opinion?*

When you call on a new prospect for the first time, <u>it is important</u> <u>for you to learn as quickly as possible how he thinks about your product</u> or <u>service *in terms of his own interest.*</u>

Probably the best way is to ask him directly. For instance, an insurance man opens the interview by asking, "How do you look at life insurance, Mr. Prospect? As something to provide for your family when you die, or as a means of financing your retirement?" A premium salesman calling on a food manufacturer says, "What is your opinion, Mr. Jones, of consumer contests for promoting a new product?" Perhaps he has never tried them, but holds strong views on the subject, or he considers them unsuitable or too expensive for his type of operation, or he ran a contest two years ago and it was an expensive flop. In addition to providing you with a valuable clue to his thinking, such an approach will make him feel that your purpose is not so much to make a sale as to solve a problem.

Identify Him by Name

Most of us recall the pleasant surprise we experienced when we happened to encounter a salesman whom we had not seen for some time and he greeted us by name. This is especially true if the name is unusual or easily mispronounced.

But all too often the man who has the best opportunity to learn the name will neglect the chance to use it effectively. When you hand your doctor's prescription to the pharmacist, he has your name right before him and it would be a simple matter for him to ask how it is pronounced. And the next time you came in to make a purchase you would feel complimented if he greeted you by saying, "Good morning, Mr. Jacoby, what can I do for you?"

A shoe salesman for one of the top stores on Fifth Avenue has hundreds of customers, most of whom he can identify by name. Occasionally he may forget the name of some lady he has not seen for quite a long time. But when she hands him her charge plate, he makes sure to take a quick look so he can say, "It has been a pleasure to serve you again, Mrs. Mittendorf."

GET IT RIGHT THE FIRST TIME

Howard Hall had just completed the installation of an attractive electric sign for a dry cleaning establishment. While he and the proprietor, John Davis, were giving the job a final inspection, a neighboring merchant strolled over to take a look.

The dry cleaner introduced him to Hall, who caught the name as Joe Holiday. The three men engaged in a friendly conversation, which was cut short by the arrival of several customers.

Next morning, Hall telephoned Mr. Davis to inquire, "When you introduced me to your friend Joe yesterday, I wasn't sure that I caught the name correctly—was it Holiday? Seems like a fine fellow."

"Yes, he's a very successful man. His name is Holloway. He owns the Colony Hardware Store on the next corner. He told me this morning that he's adding a big display room for household appliances. And by the way, he likes our new sign."

By taking the trouble to make sure of addressing Mr. Holloway correctly, Howard Hall picked up other important information which put him well on the way to another fine sale.

TALK THE PROSPECT'S LANGUAGE

An ambassador who knows the language of the country to which he is accredited has a much better chance of being understood and believed than if he must speak through an interpreter. Similarly, the business ambassador who has a ready command of his prospect's language will find a quicker response to his sales message.

A middle-aged lawyer enrolled for a course at a New York school of art and design, in which most of the other students were between 20 and 35 years of age. He explained that he wanted to become familiar with the nomenclature of the advertising business because he had so many clients in that field.

A sales representative for a pharmaceutical manufacturer must be completely competent to "talk the doctor's language" when he calls to introduce a new product, or to discuss a new approach to some medical problem. A salesman calling on retail storekeepers should be fully conversant with stock turnover, inventory control, point of purchase advertising displays, and all the other terms that make up the "retailer's language."

Learn to speak clearly, accurately and convincingly in your prospect's language.

PUT YOURSELF IN HIS SHOES

One of the oldest and best pieces of advice to salesmen is "Put yourself in the prospect's place." And still there are far too many salesmen who seem to think this merely means to show or explain the product, and then glibly add, "It's the very best buy on the market. I use it myself." Many propects might consider that to be the poorest possible reason for buying it.

What is important to one buyer is less important to the next. Each has its own problem. Only by finding out what your prospect wants or needs, and then identifying yourself with his special situation, can you possibly hope to persuade him that you are looking at it from his viewpoint.

A salesman of air-conditioning units decided to improve his sales talk, especially in terms of YOU. He began by writing down a list of all the desirable features he had to offer. Then he tried to devise "you phrases" for each one so that he could meet every type of prospect on the most favorable ground. For example:

> COMFORT. When it's hot and sticky outside, you will enjoy the comfort of your own home instead of fighting your way through traffic to the beach. You will be grateful for a really good night's sleep instead of getting up at all hours, trying to find a breeze on a hot night.
>
> HEALTH. You know that many of your family's illnesses can be traced to extremes of heat and cold. This unit is adjustable so you

can easily maintain the most healthful atmospheric conditions inside your home, no matter what the weather is outside. You will work better, use up less energy, feel fresher and more relaxed than ever before.

VALUE. You will appreciate how little electric current is required for this model. The sturdy construction assures you of low-cost maintenance, in addition to the company's iron-clad service guarantee. Your investment in this equipment will pay you good dividends for years to come.

From time to time, additional advantages of using your product or service will become known to you, either through your company or from your own customers, thus enabling you to add to your store of helpful suggestions for your prospect. Try to translate these into "you phrases" which can be employed to identify yourself with your customer and his problems.

FIND OUT WHAT'S ON YOUR PROSPECT'S MIND

Bill Dawson, sales representative for a leading investment firm, had been assigned to call on one of the largest insurance companies in America.

His manager told him, "John Swiggett, the financial vice president, is one of the most astute bond buyers in this country. Don't ever try to buck him when he starts to express an opinion. He's been on that job for nearly 40 years, and he probably knows more about this business than the next 40 bond salesmen who talk to him."

So when Bill made his first call he introduced himself to Mr. Swiggett by asking him a question. "I understand you have made a special study of the railroad situation. Most insurance companies, I realize, hold their bonds to maturity. But once in a while something may happen which makes you feel that a particular security is no longer suitable for your company to hold. Does that happen often?"

Mr. Swiggett got out a map from a file behind his desk and asked Bill, "What do you know about this railroad?"

"Not a great deal right now, but I'd be glad to look into it for you."

Swiggett shook his head. "I've been over every mile of that track. I know as much about it as that new president they installed last year. It's a fine property. We own a half million of the underlying first mortgage bonds. But they are selling at an artificial premium in this market. We might be tempted to switch into an equally sound issue whose price is not supported by such a technicality. Think it over."

Returning to the office, Bill Dawson consulted his file of the latest investment portfolios of various institutional buyers of securities. One of these was a savings bank which owned a block of the railroad bonds Mr. Swiggett had referred to. A discreet inquiry of the bank president revealed that a recent meeting of the finance committee had discussed the desirability of increasing its holding of bonds instead of putting more money into real estate mortgages.

Not long thereafter Bill's firm concluded two interesting transactions: the purchase of the insurance company's block of railroad bonds, and the subsequent sale to the bank which was restricted to the purchase of "savings bank legals."

It pays to inquire about your customers' attitudes concerning changes in styles, buying habits, economic trends and other criteria, and then fitting your sales approach to their personal predilections.

"The Song Is YOU"

Most people have a favorite salesman or saleswoman with whom they like to do business.

Mrs. Wheeler always buys her shoes at Lord & Taylor's because "Miss Johnson knows exactly what I like, and if she hasn't got it in stock she will ask me to wait until she can get it for me." Her husband buys his suits at Saks Fifth Avenue: "As long as Tony Carlson works for them, they are sure of keeping my trade. He knows what I ought to wear better than I do myself." When Mr. and Mrs. Wheeler go to the theatre, they like to eat at a little place on 55th Street, where Karl and Katy take special care of them. "They know just the things we like to eat and drink. And they often have some special suggestion, something they feel we will be happy to try—and we usually do!"

As Will Rogers is reputed to have said, "If you're trying to sell me something, make it so you'd rather be the man who bought it than the man who sold it."

What Would You Have Done?

Joe Jordan represents one of the leading distributors of mutual funds in the country. He has earned a solid reputation for putting himself in every prospect's shoes before recommending a specific issue for his consideration.

He is also an expert sales strategist, which means that he is often called upon to handle some difficult problem which another salesman has not been able to solve.

One morning his sales manager called him into his office and handed him a letter, which had been typed on the stationery of a midtown Manhattan hotel.

It was an inquiry about the firm's recent advertisement offering a booklet about mutual funds. The manager said to Joe, "I know what will happen if I give this to one of the other men. They will just telephone the hotel and ask for Mr. Barton. And if they are lucky enough to reach him, he will probably say that he will read the booklet when he has the time, and that he will get in touch with us if he is interested. Let's see what you can do with this."

If you were in Joe Jordan's shoes, *What Would You Have Done?*

(*see* page 181)

10

MAKE IT
HARD TO GET
—EASY TO BUY

One of the most common traits of human nature is the desire for something that is hard to get. This almost universal hankering of people for whatever is "hard to come by" has been skillfully exploited by salesmen of high and low degree.

When the first stainless steel razor blades, manufactured by a British sword maker, were introduced in the New York market, hardware merchants and other distributors displayed signs reading, "Only one package of Wilkinson Sword Blades to a customer." Instantly hundreds of men who had plenty of unused blades in their bathroom cabinets at home decided they wanted Wilkinsons.

Retail salespeople sometimes help a hesitant customer reach a decision by casually remarking "The Only One We Have Left."

Ever since their marriage ten years ago, Fred had been promising Nancy a fur coat for Christmas. But somehow it seemed that whenever Fred got his year-end raise, some unexpected family expense would intervene to use it up. And so the good old cloth coat was altered and made to do for another season.

Finally one November, Fred brought home a check for $1,000.

"It's a bonus from the boss," he told Nancy proudly. "That new idea I suggested for the shop is making money for the company. And I'm getting a nice raise besides. Now you're going to have your fur coat— tomorrow! I'm taking the day off to go shopping with you."

Next morning the two of them set out to visit three fur shops whose ads Nancy had been saving. "We won't spend a penny more than $500," she told Fred, "because a big piece of that $1,000 will go for extra income tax, and we ought to put the rest in the bank."

"Whatever you say is okay with me," her husband replied, "I imagine we ought to get a pretty fair coat for $500 anyway."

Their first stop was at a fashionable specialty shop. When they told the clerk they wanted to look at fur coats she took them up to the third floor. There they were introduced to Miss Gilmartin.

When Nancy told her she wanted to look at something between $400 and $450, Miss Gilmartin turned to a well-filled rack and said "These run from $395 to $500. What fur would you prefer? Let's have one of our models put this one on, just to give you an idea."

After looking at ten or a dozen coats, both Nancy and Fred were completely undecided. They had about concluded they would try another store when Miss Gilmartin turned her attention to another rack near the front of the floor. Suddenly she removed one coat from its hanger, looked at the tag, and took it to a room in the rear.

When she returned Nancy remarked, "That was a handsome coat you took back there. What kind of fur is it? May I look at it?"

"I'm sorry," said Miss Gilmartin. "That's one of our higher priced coats. I was looking through this $600 group and found that somebody had put it in the wrong place. The skins are specially matched. It's the only one we have."

Nancy insisted on seeing it.

Half an hour later, Fred found himself putting his initials on a purchase slip for Nancy's new coat—$695 plus federal tax.

Nancy hugged Fred's arm all the way home in the car. "Just what I always wanted." Fred kept his thoughts to himself. "Pretty good saleswoman, that Miss Gilmartin!"

Under such circumstances, where the prospect has only a vague idea of what the article will cost, it is natural for the buyer to hesitate before making a decision. Most people are instinctively cautious about doing something that is unfamiliar, or which reminds them of some past occurrence they regret. If the prospect has had an unpleasant experience with a fast-talking oil stock salesman, or he feels he was stuck with a bad bargain when he bought his house or his car, he will be skeptical about a salesman's urgent prodding to "buy it before it's too late."

THE CHANCE OF A LIFETIME

Norm Baxter was in the building supply business. He had lived in an apartment for several years with his wife and two children. From time to time he was tempted to consider moving to the suburbs, but his knowledge of doubtful construction practices made him hesitate.

One morning, John Jensen, builder of a new suburban development, surprised him by walking into the office instead of telephoning his order for a load of cement.

"I want to talk to you, Norm," he said, as he unrolled a set of plans. "This is the layout of my new development at Riverside Acres. I planned to build 27 fine houses on one acre plots. I've sold the 24 that are completed. Two more will be finished in a few weeks, and I have good prospects for both of them. That leaves just one plot still vacant. It's the best piece in the entire tract, and I've been saving it to build a home for my own family."

Jensen continued, "But now that the project is practically finished, we've decided to move out to Michigan, where Mary's brother Joe is an architect. Joe and I are forming a construction company to develop a 75-acre estate in a fine section near his home. After we finish that, we know of two or three other parcels which should be ready for development. . . ."

Norm interrupted his friend's enthusiastic story, "But why are you telling me all this? I'm not going to Michigan."

"Of course not," said Jensen, "but I wanted you to be the first to know that I'm not building my own home in Riverdale Acres after all. You and I have always trusted each other completely, and so I'm offering you the chance of a lifetime.

"My houses sold between $32,000 and $39,000. Mary and I drew up preliminary plans for what was to be the finest house on the entire property. I have just enough material left—lumber, bricks, plumbing fixtures and the rest—to do this one job. Since I haven't started, you could take our plans and modify them to suit your needs. You'd practically have a custom built house, the very best and the very last one available in a very desirable neighborhood."

Norm's face lighted up. "May I see the plans?"

John nodded. "Sure thing, I have them at home. Let's pick up Mrs. Baxter on the way over, and then we can drive out to the property."

And so the irresistible inducement of "something nobody else can get" turned another hesitant prospect into an enthusiastically happy owner.

It may not often be possible to present such convincing evidence of a genuine bargain, but the point to remember is that there must never be the slightest trace of misrepresentation in the transaction. It is of utmost importance that both buyer and seller emerge with confidence and satisfaction intact.

MAKE IT EASY TO BUY

Having made your proposition "hard to get" the next step is to make it "easy to buy." Now that you have aroused the prospect's desire, you must help him get what he wants.

One of the most useful words in your vocabularly at this point will be *let's*. The life insurance man says, "Let's have our doctor check you over this afternoon to see if you can get it." The automobile salesman says, "Let's see if we can get delivery in time for your vacation."

If your prospect voices or merely nods his agreement, you can usually proceed to complete the order without further interruption.

CLEAR AWAY THE OBSTACLES

Sometimes the salesman knows in advance that he must remove some physical or mental hazard before he can even gain the prospect's attention.

A remarkably successful salesman in the farm belt knew he had to catch farmers while they were at work—which is practically always. So he hired a topnotch farmhand to accompany him on his selling trips. While he talked to the farmer, the hired hand would be driving the tractor, or mending the fence, or milking the cows in the barn. Even though the salesman had been raised on a farm and could talk the farmer's language, he might not have had a chance to talk to many of his best prospects without that hired hand to take the farmer's place while they discussed the proposition.

Many people present a mental obstacle because they realize they have a need, and so they hesitate to seek information for fear of being talked into a hasty purchase. They feel reassured when told "there is no obligation."

The owner of a used car lot runs a modestly worded ad instead of the customary blatant spread. It reads, "Only two, small, timid salesmen on duty." Proprietors of gift shops and book stores encourage "browsing," but are alert to offer assistance to people who appear to have difficulty in finding what they want.

SELLING ON THE BUDGET PLAN

One of the most significant factors in the development of the American economy since the war has been the spectacular success of the selling slogan, *Buy Now and Pay Later*. It cannot be denied that the rapid rise in our standard of living has been largely due to the fact that most things have been made so easy to buy.

Even the world's largest department store, after building an international reputation for low prices "because we sell for cash," has found it necessary to introduce charge accounts and time payments for customers who are willing to pay a little extra for the convenience of "buying out of income."

MINIMIZE THE PRICE

A corollary of this national trend toward "budget buying" has been the practice of quoting prices in monthly terms, even when the actual payment is expected to be made in a single sum.

John Smith has been in the habit of buying a leading business magazine at $1.25 a copy instead of subscribing at $10 a year. The morning mail brings him a "special offer of 18 issues for only $11.75, less than 66 cents a month."

Mrs. Smith looks through the real estate ads on Sunday morning and shows her husband the picture of an attractive suburban cottage. The heading reads, "You pay only $119 a month."

When the Smiths bought their automobile, they turned in their old car and signed up for monthly payments of $38.75.

And when John Smith himself, who sells life insurance, is asked about the cost of a program he has been recommending to a client, he doesn't quote the annual premium of $710. He calls it "$60 a month or a little less than $15 a week." And if the prospect says that's too much to add to his current budget, John asks him to name any figure between $5 and $15 a week that he feels he can afford, and then proceeds to trim the program to fit that budget.

Later on, when the incidental details have been put on paper, John can offer him the discount for paying the premium annually or semi-annually in advance.

It's much like starting an automobile from a complete standstill. The salesman starts in low gear before slipping into high.

What Would You Have Done?

Brad Benson had always driven a Buick. Usually he traded in his cars every two years, when the original tires began to show signs of wear.

Jack Loomis, his regular dealer, was also a good friend who lived near the Bensons. Jack had been wondering when Brad would be dropping around to discuss a new car, so when Mrs. Benson drove their Buick into the dealer's service area for some minor adjustment, he decided to open up the subject.

"When are you and Brad going to let me show you our new model? It's nearly four years since you bought this car. It still looks wonderful, so I can offer you an attractive deal any time you say."

Grace Benson shook her head. "No, I'm afraid we've been spoiled with this grand old Buick. Best car we ever owned. All our friends admire it, and Brad is so in love with it he treats it like a favorite child. Besides, we like the lines of our car better than any of these fancy new models. Maybe you'll have something we like better next year."

After she drove off, Jack did some deep thinking. Grace Benson's comment could mean they might suddenly decide on buying another make of car instead of waiting.

Well, if you were in Jack Loomis' shoes, *What Would You Have Done?*

(*see* page 182)

11

HOW TO
START
THE ORDER BLANK

A very successful sales organization has a blackboard on the office wall listing the names of all junior salesmen, followed by squares for each day of the week. Every evening, each man is required to fill in the number of times he "spoiled an order blank" that day. In this way the men are taught to remember that you can't finish a sale unless you get it started.

Keep the Order Pad in Plain Sight

Salesmen in many lines recognize that their strongest tool is the order blank. While removing samples from his kit, or the pamphlets from his brief case, the experienced man places his order pad within easy reach so that he can begin jotting down details while the discussion proceeds.

The retail furniture salesman writes down the number of that overstuffed couch when Mrs. Jones exclaims, "That would look lovely in front of the fireplace." And if she raises no objection at that point, he may quietly ask, "Let's see—what is your address again?"

If the Prospect Balks

New salesmen are sometimes fearful of bringing the order blank out too soon. They are afraid the prospect will object by saying, "Put that away. I haven't said I'm going to buy anything." The experienced man simply says, "This is my information pad. I've just noted the size (or color or model, etc.) of this one you like. Now here we have another. . ."

Since a variety of details will need to be settled before a final decision is reached, the prospect accepts this explanation and follows the salesman's lead.

One Step at a Time

Phil Prentiss is a successful carpet salesman in a leading furniture establishment on Fifth Avenue. Mr. and Mrs. Carter seem to have a pretty definite idea of the kind of floor covering they want for their living room, having shopped a number of other stores without coming to a decision.

Among the various points to be considered are color, pattern, quality and, of course, price. After examining a dozen or more rugs, Mrs. Carter says, "I like that Venetian Brown very much. But the pattern is too prominent." The salesman has a form handy on which he enters a number under "color."

He explains that there is a somewhat similar pattern available in a slightly heavier quality. Mrs. Carter nods approvingly when a sample rug is presented for her inspection, and the salesman makes another mark on his pad. But her husband frowns at the higher price tag. He finally asks for the approximate cost of covering a floor measuring 26 feet by 14 feet 8 inches, wall to wall.

While Phil is busy with his calculation on the edge of the form, Mr. Carter notices it has a printed heading, Purchase Order, which causes him to remark, "We haven't said we are ready to buy." Phil smiles as he explains, "I just use these to jot down the information." Then he says, "That would come to about $350 in this better quality. Now let me show you one more over here. . . ."

By nailing down two or three of the several factors necessary to a final choice, Phil Prentiss has helped to guide Mr. and Mrs. Carter toward a satisfactory selection.

Take It Easy

A veteran salesman, known for his skill in closing says, "I like to play it loose. I usually have my hands behind my back when somebody walks into the showroom and starts looking around. I have my order book sticking out of my side pocket where I can reach it easily. I know that this prospect would not have come into our place unless she wanted to buy something, so I proceed on the basis that I want to send her away happy with what she bought. When I ask if I can help her, I mean exactly that. And when I write something down in my book she knows I can cross it out if we find something she likes better. The important thing is to keep it from *looking* important."

KNOW YOUR KEYS AND CUES

The question method of closing is closely related to the order blank. The life insurance salesman knows which key questions on the application form he can use for "easy openers": "Is your father in good health? . . . Have you always lived here in Maplewood? . . . Do you travel much by air? . . ."

Since there is no commitment involved in these questions, the prospect does not hesitate to answer them. Nor does he object to the salesman writing down his answers as he keeps the conversation going.

With each succeeding question and answer the stage is gradually set for the salesman to ask, "How does Mrs. Johnson spell her first name?" or "How would you want to pay for this, once a year or on the budget plan?" And so the commitment is obtained without any direct request for a major decision.

Salesmen in other lines are similarly alert for the prospect's cue that he is ready to buy. If the customer asks, "When can you make delivery?" or "Does this come in a smaller size?" the salesman's answer is simultaneous with the entry on his order pad.

Sometimes it is necessary to prompt the prospect who remains noncommittal even after the important points have been covered. So the salesman supplies the cue: "Shall we start with six cups and saucers?" or "Do you have a charge account?"

His order pad is "at the ready" for another successful close.

What Would You Have Done?

Marjorie and Ed had announced their engagement and it was time to begin preparations for the wedding.

Several of Marjorie's friends asked her what patterns of china and silverware she would prefer to receive as wedding gifts. So she and her mother set off for a shopping trip to attempt a selection.

The choice of a china pattern proved fairly simple. But after visiting three or four shops to look at sterling flatware, Marjorie couldn't seem to make up her mind.

Miss Dalrymple, the saleslady at Smithson's, had evidently spent many years in helping young brides make this important decision, so Marjorie was happy to have her offer what seemed to be a very sensible suggestion.

Suppose you had been in Miss Dalrymple's position, *What Would You Have Done?*

(*see* page 184)

12

OBJECTIONS
—OR MERE
EXCUSES?

One of the most important differences between successful and unsuccessful salesmen becomes apparent in their method of handling objections.

Basically, it is more a difference in _attitude_ than of method. One man fears that objections will arise, and hopes he may be able to answer them. The other regards objections as normal and incidental, and has complete confidence in his ability to deal with them.

A Matter of Attitude

The inexperienced salesman, like the fledgling attorney or the young intern, will do well to observe the attitudes as well as the methods of the distinguished leaders of his profession.

When a leading member of the bar is scheduled to appear in court, the spectators are sure to include a number of young lawyers who are anxious to learn how he conducts his examination of witnesses, addresses the judge and jury and persuades them of the justice of his case.

Similarly, when a famous surgeon is about to perform a difficult operation, competition arises among the younger members of the hospital staff for the privilege of assisting in the operating room and observing the expert at work.

What impresses these learners most is the relaxed and confident bearing of the experienced practitioner, his calm assurance that he can handle whatever comes up.

There is nothing arrogant about the self-confidence of the competent lawyer or salesman. His calm manner under fire is the result of many past experiences which have taught him how to deal with most situations he will encounter.

Adopt the Right Philosophy

A leading sales executive in the office appliance field recalls an important chapter from his first lessons in salesmanship:

> I was a young bookkeeper for a somewhat old-fashioned wholesale house. One day the firm decided to buy a portable adding machine, and I became so enthusiastic about it that six months later I quit my job and went to work for the office appliance company as a junior salesman.
>
> I was placed in a training class with four or five other beginners under a very competent instructor. I enjoyed Jim Gardner's teaching, much of which has remained with me to this day.
>
> It was a ten day course and on the ninth morning I decided to ask Jim about something that had been troubling me. I told him I had been reading a lot of books and articles about selling, and one which had strongly impressed me listed the four steps in a sale as Approach, Presentation, Objections and Close.
>
> I asked him when he planned to teach us how to overcome objections. Jim smiled as he replied, "I'm never going to teach anybody how to 'overcome objections.' What's more, it's wrong to say that objections occur in every sale." And then he devoted the rest of the morning to developing the *right philosophy* about objections.

Excuses

The first thing that a salesman must understand is the difference between objections and interruptions or mere excuses.

Many people, even when they feel the product is what they want, like to take their time before making a commitment. They don't object to buying—they object to buying *now*. So they offer what seems like a sincere objection, but which is really an *excuse* for delaying the purchase.

Faint heart ne'er won fair lady, and if every suitor took seriously the polite protestations of his lovely prospect when he tried for that first kiss, there would be fewer marriages.

Your prospect expects to be courted. It just isn't natural for him to yield too readily to the salesman's invitation to buy, so he thinks up some excuse to put the matter off. And woe to the faint-hearted salesman who takes him at his word.

INTERRUPTIONS

Inexperienced salesmen often mistake interruptions for objections. They become impatient and try to "bottle up" the prospect's comment, thereby risking the danger of an explosion.

Perhaps the prospect is merely seeking information: "Does this come in a larger size?" Or he wants to clarify a point he considers important: "Will this operate on ordinary house current?" He is not objecting, but actually aiming at reaching a decision. Good salesmen welcome and encourage such interruptions and know how to turn them into closing points.

REAL OBJECTIONS

An excuse can be brushed aside or ignored. An interruption should be acknowledged by a prompt answer, or gracefully deferred by stating that the point will be covered later.

But a valid objection demands and deserves a satisfactory reply. And the more genuine the objection, the better the opportunity for the strong salesman to close the sale. Salesmen become strong, just as athletes do, by putting resistance to work.

A famous clergyman says, "Thank God for the skeptic. The man who raises serious questions wants to be convinced. And the convert who had to be convinced remains the strongest believer. He knows why he believes." "He knows why he buy."

THE DISAPPEARING OBJECTION

The reason why the good salesman encounters so few objections is because he anticipates or eliminates them *as he goes along* in his orderly presentation. He proceeds on the theory that most prospects possess incomplete or faulty information about his proposition. Very often he presents the facts so clearly and convincingly that what seemed like objections in the buyer's mind quietly disappear.

Nevertheless, many buyers require further persuasion, and the salesman needs to know in what respect his prospect remains unconvinced. He sincerely welcomes the spoken objection.

LISTEN

Since this is figuratively the crossroads of the sale, it is well to observe the familiar railroad crossing sign, STOP, LOOK AND LISTEN.

One man puts it this way: "I listen, hard, to what the prospect has to say. I let him get the objection off his chest, and never let him feel that I consider it trivial. Then I pause before replying, usually in at least partial agreement with him. I don't want to make him feel I'm trying to change his mind. Let him believe he's making the decision."

RE-STATE THE OBJECTION

The next step is to re-phrase the objection. The salesman's purpose is to let the buyer know he understands, at the same time attempting to isolate the objection as the only obstacle to the purchase.

The prospect usually expects the salesman to disagree, so the salesman takes the edge off the objection by first agreeing, and then proceeding to introduce information which the prospect has not had before or has forgotten.

YES, BUT . . .

It is not necessary to use the words, "Yes, but." The essential point is for the prospect to see that the salesman is playing fair and is really trying to help him.

For example, Mr. Executive objects, "I don't want to wear a hearing aid. Plenty of time for that when I'm a grandfather, getting ready to retire.' The salesman replies, "I know what you mean—that hearing aids are mostly for older people. But you'd be surprised how many of the young men you meet every day, men whose hearing became impaired during their war service, are wearing them without your knowing it. They enjoy the same comfort and lack of strain that you and I get out of wearing eye-glasses. Let me show you this new model. It rests behind the ear, with no button showing . . ."

Or Mrs. Housewife tells the vacuum cleaner salesman, "My ten year old cleaner is still doing a better job than the fancy one my niece got when she was married two years ago." The salesman says, "You are perfectly right. It pays to buy quality. Too many people are attracted to some new gadget because of a lower price. Many of my customers feel as you do. Mrs. Wilson let me rebuild her faithful old cleaner which she still uses for heavy duty. And she also finds many lighter jobs can be done quickly and quietly with our new Electric Brush. Let me show you how easily . . ."

USE OPEN END QUESTIONS

An excellent way to meet objections is to reply with a question, "Where? . . . When? . . . Why? . . ."

That simple word WHY is probably the strongest tool for unearthing the real objection of even the toughest prospect.

Mr. Prospect tells the life insurance salesman, "I'm going to wait until next spring. See me around the middle of April."

The salesman asks, "Why?" The prospect says he still has five monthly payments to make on his car. The salesman says, "I understand. You say this insurance plan is just what you want for Mrs. Prospect and the children, but you cannot start paying for it until April. That's the reason you want to wait, is that right?"

The prospect nods his agreement, so the salesman starts writing the application and explains he will arrange temporary coverage for five months, so that the buyer will not run the risk of losing his insurance when he needs it most—while he is still paying off that loan. Futhermore, he points out that he will be a year older next April and will have to pay a higher rate.

The salesman has <u>turned the objection into a powerful reason for buying immediately</u>. And since the buyer admitted this was his only objection, he takes him at his word instead of waiting for him to think up another objection or excuse.

MAKE A LIST

An old-time salesman of heavy hardware declares that there just isn't any objection to which he cannot furnish from five to a dozen convincing answers. He says:

> Ever since I began selling, I've kept a book called "Problems and Answers." Every time I am successful in meeting an objection, I put the answer in my book. And every time I hear some other salesman use a good answer, or read it in a book or magazine, whether it's in my own line or some other, it goes in the book.
>
> I learned long ago not to bluff if a prospect asks me some ques-

tion I can't answer. I tell him frankly, "I don't know, but I'll find out for you." And when I locate the answer, it goes in the book.

By this time I know most of those answers by heart. And I've noticed that every time I dip into that "memory file" for an answer or illustration, my sales muscles get stronger and more responsive to a similar situation in the future.

DON'T BUY THE OBJECTION

The same man mentions another point. "No objection your prospect raises will bother you unless down in your heart you really believe there is some merit in his position. Just as soon as you start to 'buy the customer's objection, you are letting him make the sale to you—that he isn't going to buy! If you find that your ammunition for meeting a certain type of objection is losing its effectiveness, go to your manager and ask him to help you find out what's wrong. Even the best of us need to have our batteries recharged now and then."

"YOUR PRICE IS TOO HIGH"

The hardest lesson for many salesmen to learn is that "people don't buy on price—they buy on value."

This is true in every line, from candy bars to skyscraper hotels. A plumbing contractor was called on the carpet by a customer who complained that his estimate was higher than those of three other bidders for the work on a new warehouse.

The plumber replied, "You know the quality of work I've always done for you. By this time you should know that good plumbing doesn't cost—it pays."

It goes without saying that a salesman must believe 100 per cent in his employer's pricing policy or he cannot sell effectively. The sales manager for one of the top appliance manufacturers tells this story:

> I stopped at a department store to see how our electric irons were being displayed and sold. I picked up a competitor's iron which was price-marked at $5.95. Then I took one of our irons marked $7.95 from the next counter and asked the clerk, "What's the difference between these two irons?" Without batting an eye she said, "Two dollars." Not one word about all the exclusive features we mention in our advertising. She probably thinks the other iron costs less because it isn't advertised!

Well, what's wrong? You may say, "Dumb clerk," but that

isn't the point. It's dumb *me*, it's dumb *you*, unless all our sales people, right down to the level of retail clerks, really *know and believe* our product delivers extra value for the extra money we ask for it.

TAKE YOUR TIME

When a prospect starts the interview by asking bluntly, "What does it cost?" it's a great temptation, and a great mistake, to become involved in a discussion of price before taking the opportunity to establish value.

The salesman may reply, "That depends on what you need. Do you give it hard wear?" or "Do you mean initial cost or eventual cost?"

A sign displayed on the wall of a leading retail establishment has a message which others might well adopt, "It is unwise to pay too much, but worse to pay too little."

TURN THE TABLES

Frequently the situation is one where the salesman can ask the prospect about the merchandise or service he sells himself: "Is your paint the cheapest, or do your customers say it's the best?" or "Is your credit reporting service known as the lowest priced in its field, or do you have a reputation for faster and more reliable information than your competitors?"

TELL THEM WHY

One top salesman explains his philosophy in this manner, "When the prospect says your price is too high, he is really saying, 'Tell me why it is so good that people are willing to pay more money for it?'"

People quickly forget what they paid for a product or a service which they remember with pleasure and pride: that beautiful grand piano, that wonderful Mediterranean cruise, the "best show I ever saw."

One of the soundest conclusions concerning this whole matter of price competition was expressed in an editorial by Robert B. Mitchell, executive editor of *The National Underwriter*. Discussing a study by the Consumers Union of comparative rates charged by life insurance companies, he wrote:

Long years of experience have proved that the typical life insurance buyer is about as cost conscious as the typical automobile buyer. He probably realizes he could get a better deal than he is getting, whether it's a life insurance policy or a car he is buying, but usually at some point short of the best possible cost he lets other considerations prevail—service facilities, the personality of the salesman, or something else having nothing whatever to do with cost. This doesn't mean that the buyer isn't aware of cost—he just feels that he is close enough to the best possible cost so he's willing to settle for the product that is being offered to him.

the actual cost
the possible cost.

What Would You Have Done?

A group of wholesale appliance salesmen attending a convention were discussing ways and means of handling the buyer who keeps bringing up some competitor's item he claims is a better buy.

Joe Donahue cited an example. "I've been trying to get an important dealer who handles three competitive brands of kitchen appliances to put in our quality line, which is frankly a little higher priced. I know some of you have been in the same boat many times. How do you handle it?"

If you were in that group of salesmen, *What Would You Have Done?*

(*see* page 184)

13

SUPPLY
ADDITIONAL
REASONS

A good general avoids throwing all his forces into the battle unnecessarily. He holds some of his best reserves in the rear to reinforce the main body of troops at the right moment.

The good salesman will include in his standard presentation a wealth of motivating reasons which should be effective in persuading the average prospect to buy. But, unless he has a reserve supply of *additional reasons* for buying, he is bound to lose out in many of his attempts to close.

Many of your most important prospects, in fact, will test your mettle by raising objections with which they have successfully resisted other salesmen's efforts to sell them.

PROSPECT'S RESISTANCE DEVELOPS SALESMAN'S MUSCLE

A long-time representative of a leading container manufacturer says, "Every time we have added some new type of container to our line, whether glass or metal or plastic, one of my best customers has usually been the last to give up the old method and switch to the new. I know in advance that he is going to buck me hard. But I recognize that the objections he raises are actually intended to make sure that he will make the right decision. He wants me to give him every bit of additional information to fortify his final judgment. He makes me empty my ammunition locker completely, and when he finally makes up his mind to buy, I find myself just that much stronger to present my case elsewhere. He helps me strengthen my sales muscles."

NEED FOR THOROUGH PREPARATION

When a lawyer is called upon to represent a client in court, he recognizes the importance of unearthing and presenting every possible shred of evidence to substantiate his argument. Very often, in fact, he will request a delay of the trial in order that he will be better prepared to win his case.

In like manner, the experienced salesman realizes that he just can't have too many reasons available for persuading his customer to buy. In addition, he may sometimes find it advisable to include counterarguments to his idea and discuss them, thereby taking the wind out of possible objections later on.

The very thoroughness of your preparation will lend extra assurance to your presentation, and very often your prospect will automatically assume that you know all there is to know about the subject and will be glad to place his confidence and business in your hands.

ALWAYS SELL THE BENEFIT

It seems almost trite to mention that the most convincing reasons for buying are the expected *benefits* to the buyer. Don't sell the product, sell the benefit.

Over 100,000 quarter-inch drills were sold in this country last year. Yet none of those buyers wanted a quarter-inch drill. They wanted the holes that could be drilled with them. When a man pays $95 for a new camera instead of $59.50 for another, it is because he has been persuaded he will obtain *better pictures*.

Everything for which people spend their money, whether it's a spool of thread, a typewriter ribbon or a $100,000 machine tool for stamping automobile parts, is purchased for the *benefit* it will bring the buyer. And yet . . .

J. Porter Henry, Jr., president of the management consulting firm bearing his name, has frequently deplored the fact that salesmen—not only beginners but many seasoned veterans—overlook or forget the importance of stressing *user benefits* in their sales presentations. He says:

It may be hard to believe, but when members of our staff accompanied over 100 salesmen making their calls in the field, more than 40 per cent were found to have omitted any reference whatever to the *benefits* the buyer would receive from acquiring the product or service which was being offered.

On another occasion we made 72 calls on retail dealers with four different salesmen, and on only four calls did the salesman mention any benefit to the dealer of handling the product in question.

DEVELOP TACTICAL SKILL

As in the military field, the salesman's success depends very largely on his skill in handling the forces at his command. He must have complete knowledge of his product, particularly in terms of its benefits to the buyer. All of us have witnessed the difference between the retail floor salesman who simply shows the merchandise and quotes the price, and the man in another store who knows the product inside out and is able to present a seemingly endless number of reasons why the customer will benefit by owning it.

Not only does the successful salesman carry more ammunition when he goes into action, but he employs better timing in handling it. He knows when to press his advantage, when to give ground while his opponent reveals his position, and when to strike for a decision.

Various types of prospects call for different methods of procedure. Persons in certain occupations, such as engineers and accountants, may require more statistical information than others. Some prospects, such as foreign-born workers, may not respond to appeals which have been successful with better-informed prospects. Women are more likely to appreciate such factors as style, color and beauty of appearance. And there is always the super-thrifty buyer who is willing to do without certain "frills" which the self-indulgent prospect considers indispensable. The good salesman will be alert to discover which type of ammunition will be most effective in each situation.

HANDLING THE TIMID BUYER

Most prospects have a pretty good idea of what they want, so the salesman can confine himself to presenting the most persuasive reasons for buying his particular product. In such cases it is wise to ask for the order early, keeping extra ammunition in reserve against possible need.

On the other hand, there are many people who are timid about making buying decisions, especially if they have had some unfortunate experience in the past. Also, persons whose daily occupations do not require the making of frequent buying decisions, such as teachers and professional artists, may insist on having more factual information and supporting evidence before being convinced that the purchase will prove to their advantage. Many such prospects feel the need of having plenty of reasons with which to defend their actions if questioned by their friends or associates.

VALUE OF REPETITION

The song-writer achieves popularity by skillfully repeating his musical theme, just as the advertiser gains recognition by repeating a persuasive slogan. And the successful salesman knows the value of repeating the benefits his prospect will enjoy by using his product.

One man says, "I sometimes find it necessary to repeat what I have said, but in different words. Maybe he's tuned in on AM and I'm over on FM. He doesn't like to admit that he got lost in my technical explanation of our latest refinement in reducing vibration while accelerating the speed of the motor. So I tell him how we succeeded in making it run faster and more smoothly so he will have fewer breakdowns and lower cost of upkeep."

Another says, "When my prospect indicates he is impressed by something I have told or shown him in my demonstration, like durability or precision of workmanship, I keep on repeating the point at every opportunity. I'm like the baseball players who try to 'pile up insurance runs' while they are ahead."

GIVE THEM THE OATS

Some years ago, a top salesman attributed his success to his habit of "giving them the oats." By "oats" he meant Oral Anecdotes, Testimonials and Stories.

Prospects will be more readily impressed by testimonials from nearby users of the product, from persons in the same business or profession, from people who have solved similar problems, or who have discovered some unexpected benefit.

A salesman of country club memberships, for instance, was having difficulty signing up a prospect who admitted his interest in the 27-hole golf layout but hesitated about indulging his personal pleasure to the exclusion of his growing family. Fortunately, the membership man mentioned the Clark family whose three young children made frequent use of the club tennis courts—"and when we put in a swimming pool two years ago, all three of them learned how to swim from our full-time lifeguard—in fact, young Billy won a medal in last fall's diving competition." That's all the prospect needed to persuade his own family that it would be more economical to spend their vacation at home instead of taking that expensive trip which two of the youngsters had already vetoed.

TELL HIM A STORY

The most effective anecdote is a story which furnishes a powerful motive for taking immediate action. If the story can be illustrated with a picture or news clipping, it becomes doubly convincing.

Bill Barstow had just completed an application for a $20,000 life insurance policy. When he suggested that Mr. Jones pay him a deposit so that the insurance would be placed in force immediately, the applicant said he preferred to wait until Bill brought him the policy.

Bill began leafing through his portfolio and said, "It's possible you've heard this story before. It was broadcast on one of those 'believe it or not' programs on the radio last year."

Finally he turned to a sheet comprising several photostats, including a young man's photograph, a news clipping and a check for $20,000. Bill proceeded with the story: "This young man, Bert Nelson, lived in Akron, Ohio. One evening he decided to buy a $10,000 policy from his neighbor, a salesman for our company. Fifteen minutes after signing the application, Mr. Nelson drove his car to the home of a friend with whom he planned to spend the evening. A couple of hours later, when he failed to show up at his friend's house, a call to the police station revealed that Bert had been killed in a collision with a car crossing against the light."

Bill showed Mr. Jones the news clipping with a picture of the badly smashed automobile. Then he continued, "When the police searched Mr. Nelson's pockets for identification papers, they came across a receipt for $40 which he had paid to our salesman earlier that evening. As it happened, Bert named his father and mother as beneficiaries of the policy, but they knew nothing about this until this check for $20,000, which included the double indemnity benefit for accidental death, was delivered to them in Cleveland by our local representative."

Mr. Jones was visibly moved. And when Bill suggested that he do the same thing for his family that young Mr. Nelson had done for his parents, he merely asked, "How much do I have to pay you now?"

PERSONALIZE THE EVIDENCE

A handwritten letter addressed to the salesman provides more convincing testimony than a printed or typewritten copy. So does a snapshot he has taken himself.

A builder who specializes in remodeling old houses helps his prospects visualize the finished job by showing them "before and after" pictures he has taken of work he has done for others. Interior decorators and landscape architects often use the same method to personalize their proposals.

MELTING THE ICE-BOUND PROSPECT

Sometimes a tough prospect who has been putting up resistance for a long time will finally capitulate when confronted with irrefutable evidence that the new product is actually more efficient or more economical than the one he has clung to for years. Usually there is one "key reason" which finally unlocks the sale. Don Blake, electric appliance executive, relates such an instance from his early days as a salesman of home refrigerators:

It's hard to believe now, but many otherwise intelligent people actually thought that "electric ice boxes" were an expensive fad which would never gain popular acceptance. One of my prospects was a banker who permitted his wife to buy every kind of labor-saving device that would relieve her of unnecessary housework—except an electric refrigerator. Mrs. Thompson really wanted it, but her husband was adamantly opposed to spending a couple of hundred dollars for a service which Tony the ice-man had been performing satisfactorily for $2.40 a week.

Finally the day arrived when Mrs. Thompson had to tell her husband that Tony had gone out of business. But before he could scout around for another iceman she unloaded all the "reasons why" which she had been saving up from the information we had given her.

She told him, "We have been paying Tony $2.40 a week to keep our ice box filled. Sometimes we're not home when he comes, so he leaves it on the back porch and it's half-melted by the time we return. This usually happens when we have a big party planned for the week-end. And then there's that drip pan which somebody has to remember to empty before it floods the kitchen floor."

Then came the key reason: "Speaking of parties, we'll be glad to have those automatically frozen ice cubes instead of messing around with an ice pick just as the guests arrive." Seeing her husband wavering, Mrs. Thompson followed up enthusiastically, "Let's buy an electric refrigerator and put $2.40 in a jar every Monday—we'll have it paid for before we know it . . ."

You won't be surprised when I tell you that Mr. Thompson became one of our best boosters—probably because he remembered all those reasons which led to his conversion.

How to Handle the Call-Back

Many salesmen make a serious mistake when calling back on a prospect they failed to close last time. Instead of making a fresh start toward arousing new interest in their proposition, they try to resume where the previous interview went off the track and so they find themselves back in the ditch.

When the advertising space salesman says, "Mr. Jones, you wondered last week about our circulation in Illinois . . . ," the prospect is reminded of the excuse he used to terminate that unprofitable interview and shakes his head, "Sorry, old man, this is my very busy day. Why don't you write me a letter?"

How much more effective it would have been to start the call-back interview by showing Mr. Jones something new, perhaps an advance copy of next month's issue, including the first installment of a series of articles about his type of product.

The basic rule for every call-back is to have a *new reason* for seeing a prospect. If you can't think of a new and convincing reason for him to listen, better not see him at all until you do.

One old pro is always sure of a welcome because of his intimate knowledge of his customer's business. He keeps up-to-date through the trade papers, frequently calls attention to news items his clients have overlooked, goes to the trouble of digging up answers to problems they have mentioned which are completely outside his own sphere.

People prefer to do business with this man because they have learned that it pays off in other ways than merely stocking his line of merchandise. They like it when he takes out his memorandum pad to jot down some experience they have told him about because they want to keep on getting his ideas in return. He often leaves a self-addressed post card and says, "Drop me a line whenever some unusual problem comes up."

GIVE THEM REASONS FOR REMEMBERING YOU

Ted Thatcher is a wholesale paint salesman. When Ted and Sally invited his mother to come down to Jonesboro for a week's visit in their new home, Mrs. Thatcher wondered whether Sally still served most of her meals out of the cans and frozen food cartons she bought at the super-market.

Imagine her pleasant surprise when she sat down to enjoy a delicious roast beef dinner with all the trimmings on her first evening with Ted, Sally and little Doris. "Where did you get this wonderfully tender beef?" she asked.

Sally answered, "Yes, isn't it tasty? I had the good luck to find a butcher in this town who isn't satisfied with just selling meat. Gus Meyer makes sure that his customers get the fullest satisfaction out of what he sells them. He's taught me a lot about choosing beef that is 'marbled' with fine streaks of fat. At Thanksgiving time he suggested we order our turkey the week before, so he could select the right one to suit our needs and keep it in his storage freezer until we were ready for it. Two of our neighbors go to Gus for their meat now, and he's been very helpful with cooking suggestions we might not have known about."

Ted broke in to say, "This seems to be that kind of a town. There are three hardware stores on Main Street, but George Noonan gets most of the business. He knows all his old customers, so when he spots a newcomer he makes it a point to find out all he can about him, and assures him that his delivery service will be ready to help out in any emergency. When we had our first heavy snowfall in December, I phoned him to inquire about a man who might clear my driveway, and he had a fellow bring his jeep around in fifteen minutes."

It's no accident that Ted has sharpened his own search for extra ideas and services he can give his wholesale paint distributors and retailers, which they can pass along to their customers in turn. He says, "It costs little or nothing to give your customers these *additional reasons* for buying from you instead of the other fellow."

What Would You Have Done?

Ralph Owens was a printing salesman. Ten years ago he had landed a trial order from a leading insurance company for a 12 month's run of 5,000 monthly calendar blotters. The blotters were large enough to include a colored photo-reproduction of an attractive picture above the calendar for the current month, with the name of the company and its local agent imprinted at the bottom. The cost was shared by the company and 50 selected agents who began with a year's subscription for 100 blotters a month.

The calendars proved extremely popular with both the agents and their clients, and in a few years the monthly run had grown to over 60,000 blotters, making it Ralph's most important account.

But now Ben Blake, the advertising manager of the insurance company, told Ralph he thought it was time for a change. "We're looking for something new. Frankly, we are considering another type of reminder advertising which we can buy at a much lower cost, both to the company and our participating agents. I'm not at liberty to tell you what this other item is, but it is not in the printing line. Of course, if you have something to offer at a lower price we will be glad to consider it."

If you were in Ralph Owens' shoes, *What Would You Have Done?*

(*see* page 186)

14

ENTHUSIASM

Many good men who might have become outstanding salesmen have decided against a selling career because of a mistaken belief that it is necessary to be a show-off or an exhibitionist in order to be a successful salesman.

Quite the contrary. Enthusiasm, which the dictionary defines as "ardent zeal or interest," is an essential to success in selling, but it need not take the form of extravagant gestures or strident vocal behavior. Just as there are quietly enthusiastic fishermen, chess players and stamp collectors, there are thousands of successful salesmen who convey their enthusiasm without resorting to pyrotechnical display.

What Do You Say to Yourself?

You cannot hope to be a successful salesman unless you are sincerely enthusiastic about your product, about your company, and about the benefits it will bring to your customer. Your enthusiasm cannot be a "sometime thing." It must be strong enough to withstand the honest doubts of the average man and even the outright opposition of the hostile non-believer.

A well known sales manager makes a habit of asking applicants for sales positions why they want to sell his product and why they want to sell for his company instead of the larger and better known firms in the same field. He says:

> They have to have some interest in the product or they wouldn't want to sell it. I want to know what that interest is and where it came from.
>
> Love at first sight doesn't always bloom into the real thing. Sure, I want my new man to start out with the conviction that he is selling a superior product made by a good company. But how about later on, when the glamor of early romance comes up against the stern realities of everyday life—when he finds that prospects regard his wonderful product and his wonderful firm as quite average and ordinary?
>
> Will his enthusiasm wilt under the fire of customer-indifference and doubt? Or will he remain true to his first love by reminding himself of the reasons for his earlier infatuation?
>
> If his enthusiasm begins to wane, will he put the blame where it belongs? The product is the same, the company is the same, maybe the change is in himself! Then comes the critical question: *What does he say to himself?*
>
> If he admits the slightest doubt in his own mind, he'd better quit trying to convince others about his proposition until he can go back and revive his own beliefs. And if he can't do this, he'd better quit the job altogether.

ENTHUSIASM MUST BE CONTAGIOUS

Your enthusiasm must be genuine and it must be contagious. You must be red hot in order to make your prospect lukewarm. And after you have kindled the fire you have to keep blowing it into a bright flame. David N. Mercer, General Agent, John Hancock Life Insurance Company, Grand Rapids, Michigan, provides the following illustration:

> It is my belief that the art of salesmanship does not vary with the product. Last evening I observed a man who displayed more salesmanship than anyone I have seen in a long while. First, he discussed the general problem. He did it in a conversational tone with a simplicity that was something to behold. Then he discussed the specific problem in terms of the individual. Following this, he offered the ideal solution to the specific problem. He described it fully and accurately, with a minimum of extraneous words and clichés.
>
> Then he proceeded into the close. Talk about a man being a strong closer! This man literally had people out of their seats. He believed in his message, and in what it would do for his prospects. His enthusiasm and conviction were positively contagious. His name was Billy Graham.

Keep the Fire Hot

Once you have brought your prospect's enthusiasm to the boiling point, don't let him cool off. Aim for action now. Delaying until "some other time" means you will have to bring his enthusiasm up to 212 degrees all over again. Meanwhile, he will have lots of opportunity to cool off altogether.

Your greatest obstacles are the prospect's inertia, indifference and procrastination. Your best weapon for overcoming these will be your unflagging enthusiasm.

One top salesman says, "The biggest kick I get out of my job comes from the belief that my prospect will be grateful for having bought it. My belief and interest may not come out with a whoop and a holler, but the client will recognize them, he will feel their presence, he will be more likely to buy because they are there. It's exciting for me to land an order, of course, but I want the buyer to be just as excited about his purchase as I am."

Enthusiasm Banishes Nervousness

An appliance salesman confessed to his supervisor, "I have a peculiar mannerism of wetting my finger tip when I get going in my demonstration. I've been told so often to watch this that it makes me nervous." His supervisor laughed, "The best antidote for any kind of nervousness is to generate real enthusiasm about what you are offering and get the prospect excited. Then both of you can have as many mannerisms as a cageful of monkeys and neither will notice it in the other."

A successful sales manager confesses to an embarrassing chapter in his early experience as a salesman:

> When the Stenotype Company first introduced its machine some years ago, it decided to market it through the business colleges and secretarial schools. When parents brought their youngsters to enroll for shorthand courses they were shown the new "machine way in shorthand," and a representative of the company tried to persuade them to buy a machine for their sons or daughters, to be paid for out of their earnings after completion of the school course.
>
> My first assignment was to spend a week in September at one of the largest schools in the metropolitan area, interviewing parents and demonstrating the machine to prospective students of stenography.

I must have had over 50 of these interviews without coming anywhere near a sale.

On Saturday morning I reported my lack of results to my district manager. To my complete consternation he directed me to listen on his secretary's telephone extension while he called up the school principal and asked for his opinion of my performance.

Dr. Robinson began by making polite excuses for the young man and saying he hoped some of the prospects would decide to buy later on. But when my manager pressed him further the principal admitted, "I was surprised to notice he never smiled. He appeared to be nervous and without much enthusiasm or conviction about the story he told."

My ears began to burn. And I was downright frightened when the conversation ended by the manager's telling Dr. Robinson that I would return to the school on Monday morning—"and you can rest assured he will do a good job for you next week."

I tried to beg off by suggesting that I try my luck at one of the smaller schools, but the manager remained firm in his decision.

During the following hour he patiently rehearsed the demonstration with me, emphasizing just two points which the principal had mentioned: the need for a Smile and Enthusiasm.

He taught me two lessons I never forgot: 'A nervous person never smiles. And an enthusiastic person is never nervous.'

On Monday morning I greeted Dr. Robinson with an enthusiastic smile. He introduced me to a Mr. and Mrs. Taylor, suggesting that I show them the "machine way in shorthand." My enthusiastic demonstration led to their daughter's enrollment the next day.

When I reported back to the office on Friday with six completed contracts, the manager told me, "Dr. Robinson just called me. He wants to have you assigned to his school for the rest of the term."

Put A Smile in Your Voice

A business executive had occasion to telephone his office from outside and was dismayed by the unenthusiastic manner in which his assistant answered the call. A few days later he called a meeting of his staff, to which he invited a telephone company supervisor who had taught hundreds of private switchboard operators that "the voice with the smile wins." A series of voice coaching lessons not only improved everybody's telephone manners but added new dimensions of enthusiasm to their personal contacts with the firm's customers, as well as with each other. One member of the group declared, "I learned how to use more enthusiastic words, and to use them more enthusiastically. It was a marvelous idea. A wonderful experience for all of us."

How to Avoid Staleness

Most of us can remember occasions when we entered a store with a half-made decision to make a purchase, only to leave without buying anything because of the listless, unenthusiastic manner of the salesperson we talked to. The more frequently a salesman tells his story the more easily it can become a mere recital of facts and figures, completely lacking in persuasive power to make people buy.

A leading actor, starring in a long run on Broadway, explained how he maintains his enthusiasm after hundreds of performances in the same role. "There may be only a handful of people in the theatre, but there is at least one person in the audience who will remember it as long as he lives."

Another actor tells of his early experience with a stage director who was internationally famous for his ability to extract superlative results from performers who had never achieved such heights of dramatic enthusiasm before:

> I remember a scene which we rehearsed repeatedly for hours on end while he coaxed, cajoled, scolded and threatened each one of us in turn in order to build more believable enthusiasm into the climactic moment at the close of the second act.
>
> Finally the stage props became so shaky from all our stomping and pounding that one of the side walls collapsed right over the head of the leading lady. Although completely unhurt, she was so wrought up that she let out a scream that could have been heard ten blocks away.
>
> The director jumped up and yelled, "You've got it, you've got it. Do it just like that on opening night and we can't lose." He was right. The rest of us caught the same emotional pitch, and the audience ate it up.

Roll Out the Red Carpet

As was said earlier, it usually isn't necessary to "hoot and holler" to obtain an enthusiastic acceptance of your performance by your audience of one. The desired effect can often be attained by careful attention to the "atmospheric details" which can make or mar your sale.

Bill Bradley, an outstandingly successful retail furniture salesman, says:

I like to sit down at my radio on a quiet evening and just concentrate my listening on the commercials. Some of them are wonderful, and others are so downright unbelievable that you wonder whether the person delivering the pitch ever used the product himself.

And then I remember those wonderful commercials that turned my timid mother, who had always been afraid of traveling by air, into such an enthusiastic booster for the X.Y.Z. Airlines.

My sister had moved to Texas with her family from Long Island. Mother wanted to visit them for Christmas, but she didn't feel she could stand the strain of spending several days in an automobile or on a train. But when one of us suggested that she could fly down to Dallas non-stop, have lunch on the plane and arrive that same afternoon in time to have Ann meet her at the airport, she agreed enthusiastically.

She had been hearing on the radio about those marvelous "red carpet flights" of the X.Y.Z. Airlines, the personal attention the stewardesses were trained to give to elderly travelers, the delicious meals, the company's long record of experience and security, the smooth and trouble-free operation of the latest type of flying equipment. So she actually pictured herself enjoying such an experience some day on her own.

The happy day finally arrived, and when Ann's husband got his camera ready to snap a color picture of the arrival of Grandma's plane at the Dallas airport, there was a sure-enough red carpet rolled out for the arriving passengers to step on after their luxurious flight from New York.

So whenever I see a nice old lady, or even a middle-aged one, or perhaps a young couple who are planning their new home, walk into our display room, I look at the red carpet on the floor and say to myself that maybe they saw that attractive ad we had in the paper last Sunday or last month or even last year, and this is the day they have chosen to find out whether our furniture is as wonderful as we've been saying it is.

And then I proceed to give them the same red carpet treatment I would like to receive for myself when I go out to spend my own money for something I have wanted for a long time.

Somebody told us about a neatly lettered notice he saw tacked on the employees' bulletin board of a leading retail establishment:

EMPLOYEES WHO ARE NOT FIRED WITH ENTHUSIASM

WILL BE FIRED WITH ENTHUSIASM

The Management

What Would You Have Done?

Fred Fowler had held the bottling franchise for a leading soft drink in a small New England city for 20 years. When hé died, his son Jerry, who had tried his hand at a variety of jobs, thought he would automatically succeed to his father's profitable business.

But when he presented himself at the head office of the parent company, he discovered that three or four other candidates had already applied for the franchise.

Remembering how often his father had spoken of George Maynard, one of the company's officers with whom he sometimes went fishing, Jerry decided to plead his case with Mr. Maynard in person.

"You know how well-known the Fowlers have always been in Clarksville," he began. "Dad built up a fine reputation in the community, and we would have the same people continue to run things at the plant. Why would you think of making a change?"

Mr. Maynard was non-committal. He admitted that Jerry's father had done a good job through the years. "But there are a lot of new factors to be considered. For one thing, competition has become a lot stiffer. What experience have you had in handling food and beverage lines, Jerry?"

Jerry admitted he had a lot to learn, but felt confident that with the assistance of his father's competent staff he would be able to maintain the leading position in the territory. "You won't be sorry, Mr. Maynard. Better stick with the Fowlers instead of taking a chance on some unknown newcomer."

If you were in George Maynard's shoes, *What Would You Have Done?*

(*see* page 187)

15

MOTIVATION

One of the most common excuses offered by unsuccessful salesmen is that the prospect "isn't in the market." Of course he isn't. Not like the house-wife who suddenly becomes aware that she is out of coffee or sugar. Not like her husband who discovers he is fresh out of razor blades, or his gas tank is nearly empty, or he needs a new commutation ticket.

All of us spend money for our daily necessities as they arise, without the aid or prompting of a salesman. But we don't confine our buying to the things we *need*. Most of our spending is for those goods and services, and for specific brands, which we have been motivated to *want*. We didn't wait until we were "in the market" for them, nor did the salesmen who helped us to decide to buy them.

MOTIVATION vs. LOGIC

John and Jerry were roomates at college. During senior year they were interviewed by the personnel director of a large manufacturer of household appliances. Both were hired, and after six months of preliminary training John was assigned to the accounting division and Jerry to the sales department.

Two years later, John's wife remarked that his friend Jerry seemed to be making faster progress and more money than he. So John asked to be transferred to the rapidly expanding sales division.

Assigned to an outlying suburban territory, John proved a sad disappointment to himself and to his manager. When asked what seemed to be the trouble, John reported, "Most people tell me they aren't in the market."

Further discussion revealed that John was relying chiefly on the logical points he considered most important, such as quality, economy and durability, instead of stressing such basic emotional appeals as comfort, safety, convenience, health, simplicity and ease of operation.

John's manager pointed out that an appeal which seems important to the salesman may not appear so to the prospect; that different prospects buy for different reasons and respond to different emotions.

"A good presentation," he concluded, "will include both reason *and* emotion, not reason *or* emotion."

BASIC EMOTIONAL APPEALS

Almost any salesman can improve his effectiveness by making a list of the emotional appeals he might employ in presenting the merits of his product. Such a list would probably include some of the following:

ambition	appearance	beauty	cleanliness	comfort
convenience	contentment	economy	fear	good taste
health	love	luxury	pleasure	prestige
pride	profit	recreation	refreshment	safety
security	simplicity	speed	status	style

The successful salesman knows how to translate logical reasons for owning his product into emotional impulses to acquire it *now*.

WHY DO WE BUY?

The instructor of a "brush up course" in salesmanship asked his students to bring to their next class a list of the last ten purchases made by themselves or members of their families. Here are some of the experiences they reported:

Jack B. stopped at a haberdashery to buy some shirts. The clerk called his attention to a sale of pajamas. He bought two pair, also a couple of ties he didn't really need. And a novelty tie clip. (Motivation: personal appearance)

Phil G. asked his wife to call the telephone company to repair the dial on their bedroom extension. When he got home he found she had been persuaded to pay a little extra for the new Princess set with a dial that lights up in the dark. (Motivation: convenience, safety)

Jim D. bought a pair of tickets for a musical comedy theater party for the benefit of a local charity. (Motivation: benevolence, pleasure)

Joe M. stopped to buy some batteries and a cord for his hearing aid. The consultant had him try out the new cordless model attached to his eye-glasses. Joe bought it. (Motivation: appearance, convenience)

Arthur K.'s wife went to her shoe shop to buy a pair of her favorite walking shoes, "the only last that doesn't make my feet hurt." The saleslady told her, "You are lucky. We have just two pair left in your size. When the next shipment comes in, the price will be higher." Mrs. K. bought the two pair. (Motivation: comfort, economy)

MOTIVATIONS CHANGE

Not only will different prospects respond to different emotional appeals, but the same prospect will respond to different motives at different times.

Parents will put their personal interests and desires aside while their children are growing up, in order to provide comforts and necessities for their youngsters. Later on, they will feel free to satisfy their postponed desires for things they formerly felt they could not afford.

Changes in style, public attitude and economic conditions have an important effect on the sale of clothing, house furnishings, automobiles and forms of recreation. During the long depression, salesmen of Cadillac cars and other luxury items found that many prospects felt self-conscious about displaying their wealth. More recently, the compact car has caught the fancy of many people who could readily afford a larger and more expensive vehicle. The young go-getter on his way up the social ladder responds to the artificial status appeal. The man who has already arrived attaches more importance to satisfying his personal tastes.

TIME BRINGS CHANGES

Emotional appeals also change with the seasons. People want to keep warm in the winter, cool in the summer (comfort). They buy skates and skis in November, golf clubs and tennis rackets in May (recreation). They buy greeting cards and gifts for family and friends for Easter, Christmas and other seasonal occasions (love and affection); also new shoes, hats and other accessories for themselves (appearance and luxury).

Travel agencies, railroads, airlines and hotels gear their sales campaigns to the seasons and to such special events as conventions, sports and the World's Fair (recreation, pleasure).

Music shop owners know that radio and hi-fi enthusiasts buy the latest recordings of concert artists and other entertainers while their popularity is high (pleasure, status).

A tropical storm which wrought heavy destruction in a New England city also created a timely opportunity for builders, painters and other contractors to persuade real estate owners to restore and improve properties which had become neglected eyesores in the area (civic pride, profit).

An insurance salesman found that many of his neighbors and friends became interested in reviewing their policies for disability and double indemnity coverages after two leading members of the community were involved in a fatal accident (fear, security).

Good salesmen are alert to time their appeals to fit changing conditions or circumstances when prospects are apt to be most responsive.

The Personal Touch

Personality traits such as friendliness, forthrightness, integrity and good manners play an important part in the salesman's ability to arouse emotional response. This is equally true with hesitant first-time buyers and established repeat customers.

A housewife had maintained her personal checking account for many years at a local bank where she was on friendly terms with everybody from the doorman to the vice president. When she moved to a town twenty miles away she remained a loyal customer of the bank, despite the inconvenience of distance and occasional bad weather. Such deep-seated customer loyalties are not easily shaken or transferred elsewhere.

People instinctively feel that they "want to get their money's worth." A lawyer who had been told by his doctor to stop smoking had a habit of stopping at a confectioner's for a half-pound of gum drops to munch whenever he "felt the urge."

Almost without realizing it, he began to favor one of the salesclerks who always placed a partly filled box of the candy on the scale and then kept adding more pieces until the scale was tipped. The other girls usually started with a box already full and then took away two or three pieces to balance the scale.

Use Imagination to Stimulate Emotions

A life insurance man says, "You know, doctor, your wife might be better off if you were a grocer. She might be able to run a grocery store, or sell it for a good price if anything happened to you. But she couldn't possibly continue your medical practice or sell it to somebody else."

The same man begins his retirement income presentation by taking out a blank sheet of paper and very deliberately writing out a number: 12,648. He passes the paper to his prospect who invariably asks, "What's that?"

The salesman replies, "That represents the number of meals you will have to buy after age 65 if you live a normal expectancy. If you could get them for just $1.00 each, you would need $12,648 and so would your wife. Are you sure of having $25,000?" By this time the prospect's emotional response has been fully prepared for the salesman's suggestion to do something about it.

Another insurance man sells disability coverage by reaching into his pocket and spreading a few $100 bills on the table, saying, "Mr. Jones, if you were forced to stop working by illness or an accident, how many of these would you need per month?"

Motivating the Purchasing Agent

What has been said about selling directly to prospects for their own use and enjoyment applies equally well to persuading a purchasing agent who interviews hundreds of salesmen.

Philip H. Gustafson, in a recent article in *Nation's Business*,[1] quotes John J. McCarthy, Consultant in Sales Training and Practices for General Electric:

> Salesmen used to contend that people don't buy turbines and defense systems on the basis of emotion. I've always maintained that they do. Many a big purchaser has gone to the opposition because he thought the salesman wasn't giving him enough personal attention.

The salesman calling on retail merchants, jobbers and industrial accounts must remember that general buying policies are set up by the

---

[1] Philip H. Gustafson, "Let Emotions Help You Sell," *Nation's Business*, October, 1961.

companies he is trying to sell, but that actual purchasing decisions are made by individuals in their employ. The purchasing agent responds to the words and actions of the salesman in the same way when he buys for his employer as he does when he is buying for himself.

A Man with Whom People Like to Do Business

Joe Plunkett is the purchasing executive for a wholesale distributor of commercial refrigerators. His firm handles four leading makes of refrigeration units, but Joe has fallen into the habit of favoring one manufacturer; not because of any marked difference in the price or quality of the product, but largely due to the trouble-shooting skill of their salesman, Bill Dunn. Joe says:

> I don't know what I'd do without his help whenever we get in a jam. I remember the hot summer night I had to telephone Bill to pacify the owner of a supermarket who reported that the refrigeration unit in his meat storage room had gone completely out of order. I told Bill, "I hate to ask you to come all the way out here at this hour, but this man Owens is really seeing red. He was leaning toward another make when we persuaded him he would be happier with yours at the time he built his new market last year. Now he's so mad he says he'll get the hospital board to cancel the contract we landed for supplying the refrigeration and air-conditioning for a new three-story wing."
>
> Bill hurried out to the scene of the trouble and quickly discovered that the fire department had turned off the electric power while extinguishing a blaze in a drug store directly behind the meat market. After making sure that the power had been restored, Bill presented himself at the office of the owner and asked if he could use the telephone to head off the truck which was already on the way with an emergency unit, "just in case."
>
> Then he showed Mr. Owens how he could add to the attractiveness of his dairy department and actually save floor space by installing a new display case unit we had been trying to sell him without success. So Bill ended up by landing a nice order for us, in addition to saving our valuable contract with the hospital.

Romance

Good salesmen know how to "romance" about the goods and services they offer to their prospects. They paint word-pictures of the benefits their fortunate buyers will possess, anticipate the pleasures they will enjoy.

A great salesman explained why he preferred his job to any other:

"The salesman is the one who makes people's dreams come true. He helps them anticipate the future, turn today's visions into tomorrow's realities. He helps them fulfill their desires, satisfy their yearnings. He shows them how to become happier, healthier, more prosperous and secure, loved by their families and respected by their friends."

This man has at different times been successful in selling life insurance, automobiles, real estate and investments. As an insurance agent he helped fathers who had never been to college guarantee a higher education for their children, and to assure home buyers who hesitated at signing up for 25 years of monthly installment payments that his company would make their homes financially free and clear in case of unexpected disaster.

As a real estate man, he leased a Scottish castle to a millionaire who had been shown through the estate by a caretaker who merely described its historic past and former occupants, but who failed to combine these features into a persuasive invitation to enjoy its present advantages and amenities.

SALESMEN OF DEMOCRACY

Dr. Ernest Dichter, president of the Institute for Motivational Research, declared in an address to the Sales Executives Club of New York:

Each time you go out and buy a new car, a new suit, a house, you base your decision on a philosophy of life. If you believe the world is heading for collapse or that the nation is on the verge of a long depression, you will buy less than if you have a more optimistic philosophy. The real defenders of a positive outlook on life, the real salesmen of prosperity, and therefore of democracy, are the individual salesmen who defend the right to buy a new car, a new home, a new radio. The salesman must sell the idea that things are going to be good, not bad. More than that, it is up to him to *make* things good rather than bad.

What Would You Have Done?

Jim and Janet Jenkins and their two children had spent 20 happy years in their comfortable home in suburban Springtown. But now that Johnny and Helen were both married the house suddenly seemed too big, the neighborhood too crowded, and the nearby highway too noisy.

Then they heard of an opportunity to buy a piece of land further out on the island where they could build a smaller cottage, where Jim would have room for the greenhouse he had long wanted, and Janet would have the privacy she desired in order to resume her interrupted writing career. But the price was a little beyond their reach. Unless, of course, they could sell their own place at a good figure.

When they put their house up for sale another difficulty arose. Every real estate broker in town said they were asking five or six thousand dollars more than other properties were selling for in that area. Newspaper ads brought equally discouraging results. When the slack summer season arrived, Janet suggested they spend Jim's vacation on a motor trip to Nova Scotia.

"But I hate to leave the house empty while we're away," said Jim. "It would be just our luck to have a buyer show up while the place is closed."

Well, if you were in their shoes, *What Would You Have Done?*

(*see* page 188)

16

IMPLIED CONSENT

A veteran appliance salesman says, "Nearly all of my sales are closed on implied consent. When I reach the point where everything has been clearly explained and the prospect raises no objection, I have the right to assume he wants to buy. So I proceed to fill out the order."

The salesman deliberately avoids asking for a forthright yes or no, because the answer will usually be "no." The prospect knows he ought to take the forward step, but without your assistance he will probably find some excuse for putting it off. By assuming the buyer's consent you are actually helping him fulfill his desire.

HELP THEM GET WHAT THEY WANT

Jack Saunders is the manager of a smart luggage shop on the main shopping street in town. He says, "I always assume that a person who walks in here has an unsatisfied desire for something he or she hopes to find. If I can help them find what they want, they will be grateful for my assistance."

A woman steps in and asks, "How expensive is that alligator handbag you have in the window?" Jack knows she would like to own that bag—if it doesn't cost too much. So he leads her to a counter on which he proceeds to place three alligator bags. "These range from $45 to $79.50. This is the brown one you saw in the window. The marking of the leather is unusually fine."

The lady picks up a large bag. "Do you have this style in a smaller size?" The salesman reaches into a lower compartment and comes up with three smaller bags which he carefully places on the counter. "Let me show you a special feature on the inside of this one . . ."

She seems to like it, opens and closes it and holds it against her suit while glancing in the mirror. She turns to examine another bag, but keeps the first one in easy reach. Then she inquires, "What are these priced at?"

The salesman helps her decide. "That last one is $49. The other one, with the secret pocket you like, is $57.50. It's a very popular style. And you can't beat alligator for wear." By this time he has removed the other bags from the counter. And when she takes another approving look in the mirror at herself and the higher priced bag, he nods his agreement and starts to fill out the sales slip.

While assuming his customer's implied consent, Mr. Saunders also compliments her on her good taste. "It's a handsome bag and a truly wonderful value. You will enjoy it for a long time." She gratefully accepts his judgment. "You have been very helpful."

Watch for Buying Signals

Closing through implied consent requires both tact and good timing. Before you can venture to take the prospect's consent for granted, he must have given some indication that he is at least partly sold on your proposition. Sometimes he will reveal his thinking by a question which can be interpreted as a "buying signal." For instance:

"Do you have this table in mahogany?"

"Could we arrange for time payments?"

"How long a guarantee do I get?"

"Where do I get service?"

Or the prospect may volunteer a statement indicating partial acceptance, such as:

"This covering looks more durable than the one we saw before."

"I like the substantial construction of this model."

"It's the same make as our dishwasher."

"It's the first I've seen that would fit in our kitchen."

An alert salesman will be prompt to point out other advantages to support the buyer's favorable impression, following up with an "assumptive close" such as:

"Do you have a charge account?"

"How soon would you want delivery?"

"Would you want to use our budget payment plan?"

THE AUTOMATIC CLOSE

Probably the simplest form of closing is the "customer's choice" or what many salesmen call the automatic close, in which the prospect closes the sale himself.

This is most easily done when the salesman has a number of sizes, ✓ colors or models to offer the prospect.

In a typical case the salesman has completed his explanation of the product and its benefits to the prospect. Then he says, "You have your choice of these five decorator colors. Which do you prefer?" Or "This is the standard size, or you may prefer the larger economy size. Which would be best for your family?" Or the salesman may ask, "Do you like this model with the high gloss finish, or would you prefer the colonial model in the dull finish?"

The customer indicates his choice and the sale is completed.

SMALL SALES TEACH CLOSING OF LARGER ONES

The sales manager of a leading furniture company offers the following illustration:

It often drives me wild to see a salesman hard at work on a prospect who could have been closed ten or fifteen minutes ago on the basis of implied consent. Some men never seem to master the art.

But Tony, the fruit peddler, does it instinctively. When a woman stops at Tony's stand and asks the price of a dozen bananas, watch what Tony does. He simply reaches for a paper bag, shoves in a dozen bananas, hands the package to the customer and says, "Sixty cents."

Many salesman, dealing in more expensive goods and services, can learn from our humble friend Tony, whose wits have been sharpened by the necessity of building his sales volume out of a lot of small transactions.

TURNING THE OBJECTION INTO A FIRM CLOSE

Tony's technique can be applied to the sale of a retirement income policy. Let's say you're an insurance salesman trying to sell a prospect who has listened attentively, nodded his agreement as you went along, and raised no serious objection. But finally he thinks of something which seems to him unanswerable.

"You say, Mr. Salesman, that this income is guaranteed to me for life, or for a minimum of ten years in any event. Since I understand that women live longer than men, my wife would be left high and dry if she lived for more than ten years after my retirement began."

So you help him make up his mind by reaching for the application form and saying, "That's an important point, Mr. Prospect, and it's all taken care of by the joint survivorship provision in the contract. Neither you nor your wife can be left without an income. And how does Mrs. Prospect spell her first name?"

When he tells you, the sale has been closed by implied consent.

It May Not Always Work

Johnny Blake was only ten, but big enough to shovel a path in the three inch snowfall in front of his house. Mrs. Gray watched him from next door, and when Johnny was finished she called to him, "That was a nice job, Johnny, will you do mine next? I'll pay you a dollar."

And next time it snowed, he went right ahead and cleared both the Gray sidewalk and automobile driveway. But when he rang the bell to show Mrs. Gray what he had done, it was her grouchy husband who opened the door. "Nobody told you to shovel our walk," he declared, "I was going to do it myself."

Johnny turned away to hide his disappointment. After the door had closed with a bang, he proceeded to shovel the snow back onto Mr. Gray's sidewalk.

When he told his dad about it that evening, Johnny got his dollar after all, together with a bit of advice, "It may not always work, son, but selling on implied consent is still a good idea."

What Would You Have Done?

Ralph Reynolds, real estate broker in a fashionable suburb, looked up and saw Mr. and Mrs. Howard getting out of their car in front of his office.

Several months ago Ralph had spent two days showing the Howards ten or twelve houses which seemed to fit most of their requirements. But whenever Mrs. Howard seemed ready to make a final decision, her husband raised a strenuous objection, "We simply can't afford to pay that much money."

Consequently Ralph was pleasantly surprised to have Mr. Howard renew their discussion by asking whether the Atwater house on Lakeview Road was still available. Mrs. Howard said, "We drove past there the other day. It's such a lovely place and a fine location. We thought it might have been sold."

Ralph got out his portfolio and turned to the page describing Mrs. Atwater's property. "I saw the owner last week. She's had a number of offers, but her price still stands at $40,000.

Mr. Howard looked non-committal. Finally he declared, "I've said repeatedly that we couldn't pay more than $35,000." When Ralph shook his head, Howard looked at his wife and said, "Mary, do you think we could possibly stretch it to 36 or 37 thousand, or . . ."

Well, if you were in Ralph Reynolds' shoes, *What Would You Have Done?*

(*see* page 189)

17

CLOSING ON
A MINOR
POINT

One of the simplest closing techniques is to obtain the prospect's agreement on a minor point and proceed to fill out the order. This method recognizes that most people find it easier to make minor decisions than major decisions.

The Minor Decision Is Painless

It happened when your wife went shopping and was undecided about which type of coffee-maker to buy. The clerk helped her by explaining that one kind turned off automatically. When he saw that she liked that one better, he filled out the order.

It happened again when you stopped to buy some white shirts but didn't know exactly what you wanted to pay. The salesman asked for your size and added, "with or without French cuffs?" When you said "with," he opened a fresh box of three shirts, took one out to show you, and said, "Our most popular brand, $4.50 each. We're having a special sale, three for $11.95. Shall I send them, or will you take them with you?" The order pad was already in action.

Good Salesmen Have a Stock of Minor Points

Salesmen in various lines have their own favorite "minor points" which they find useful in helping hesitant prospects to a final decision.

A life insurance salesman, having completed his presentation and hearing no objection, innocently asks, "If we have any correspondence with you, shall we write you at your business or residence address?" The prospect spells out his home address, the salesman writes it down and proceeds with the other entries on the application form. And the customer is relieved to find the matter is settled.

A wholesale food salesman asks his jobber prospect, "Shall we make three monthly shipments of 100 cases each, or send the whole 300 on March 1st?" The customer says, "Better send a hundred now, and I'll let you know later about the other 200."

The automobile salesman has a variety of minor point closings: "Is this the shade of green you want?" or "Would you want white wall tires?" or "Shall we include the radio, heater and clock?" The lady says, "Let's leave out the clock. And how soon could we expect delivery?"

The typewriter salesman asks, "Do you prefer the standard numerals, or would you prefer the more legible 'tail figures' like this sample?" The buyer says, "Oh, yes, these are much better for writing proposals and price quotations. Would there be an extra charge?" The salesman says there will be no charge, puts a check mark in a box on his order blank and hands it, with his pencil, to the customer for his signature.

Closing with a Crayon

A sign salesman has devised a close which he describes as "doing what comes naturally." He says, "Most of my customers are retail merchants. I prepare an attractive preliminary sketch on which I make sure to misspell the prospect's name. He picks up the black crayon which I have placed beside the sketch and corrects the spelling. He holds the crayon in his hand, looks the whole thing over carefully, and usually adds or changes something here or there. And before he's aware of it, it's *his* sign . . . and my order!"

What Would You Have Done?

Mr. and Mrs. Brown go out to replace a couple of shrubs on their property which have died over the winter. They are thinking of spending $25 or $30 but it soon becomes apparent that they will have to pay a little more.

Mrs. Brown is enthusiastic about a nicely shaped Japanese Holly. She asks, "Do you have a pair of slightly smaller ones?" The salesman answers, "You'll be better off starting with one good one like this, instead of a couple of little ones that will take several years to develop."

Mr. Brown frowns and asks, "How much would this one cost?"

If you were the salesman, *What Would You Have Done?*

(*see* page 190)

18

TAKE
COMMAND

A sales training instructor was telling his class about an incident which occurred when he was twelve years old.

"One of my pals and I spent an afternoon at the amusement park. We used up most of the rides and shows on our combination ticket, saving the best one, the 'Shoot the Chutes,' until last.

"Frankly, we had been putting it off because we were a little nervous about it. Having heard older people yell and scream as the little boat came shooting down the steep incline and hit the water with a shower of spray, we were torn between a desire to enjoy the thrill and a secret fear of the danger involved.

"Finally, we presented our tickets and climbed aboard the little car which took customers to the top of the tower, where they were transferred to their seats in the boat. While Johnny and I hung back momentarily, the other people rapidly filled up the middle seats so that the only one left for us was way up front.

"We tried to tell the attendant that we'd rather wait for the next ride, but he grabbed us by the arm and pushed us into our seats before we knew what was happening. As the boat began to move and the girls in the rear started their screaming, Johnny and I huddled together in a moment of genuine fright.

"But a few seconds later, when we hit the water and the boat bounced toward the exit ramp, we were so thrilled and delighted by our experience that we rushed back for another ride, grabbing the front seat before anybody else could."

When the instructor asked the class whether anyone remembered a similar experience, a young veteran of the Air Force recalled his first solo flight at the training base.

"All of the cadets had had hours of careful instruction, first in Link Trainers and then in dual-control planes with an instructor along. But still we couldn't help being a bit nervous because of the occasional crackups we had witnessed, sometimes by men we had considered completely fearless.

"When the morning arrived for our solo tests and we were lined up in our flying togs, each of us wished secretly that he would be the last man to be called. Sure enough, I was given the honor of leading off! No chance for ducking or pleading temporary indisposition. I was marched to the plane and given a few last-minute orders, and pretty soon I was taxiing my machine down toward the takeoff line.

"It was a bright and sunny morning, and as I soared off into the bright blue yonder, all of the nervousness disappeared in the thrill of achieving the goal I had been training for during all those weeks. I was the first cadet in our group to win his wings, and I thanked our commanding officer for letting me have the honor of showing my buddies how easy it was."

The sales instructor thanked the student and called the attention of the trainees to two important factors in these somewhat similiar experiences.

"First, somebody had to take charge of the situation in order to get the prospect to move. Second, when the move had been made the prospect was delighted with the experience and grateful to the person who had made it possible."

The Attribute Supreme

It is universally acknowledged that the one man who has exerted the greatest influence on the course of human events in this century is Winston Churchill. His supreme attribute was the ability to *take command*,

and to make others want to follow his leadership. People of high and low degree instinctively admire the men and women whose persuasive leadership has won them to their cause.

One of America's largest corporations conducted an intensive study to answer the question "What makes a good salesman?" It was found that the most important qualities were dominance, self-confidence and leadership. Conversely, it was found that men lacking these characteristics were judged unsuccessful as salesmen.

One authority has observed, "The difference between the top salesman and the fair-to-middling man is often a matter of degree in asserting his command of the situation. This is sometimes revealed in the selection of men to head trade associations, especially in the marketing and selling field. The man chosen for the presidency is likely to be one who is accustomed to taking command—and having people like it. The lesser posts are more apt to go to the steady-going guys whom everybody trusts and respects, but who are seldom found taking charge of a sticky situation."

FEELING SORRY FOR THE PROSPECT

When Bill Bullis, wholesale grocery salesman, ran into an old schoolmate, Jerry Johnson, the two men began exchanging experiences in their respective jobs.

Jerry, assistant luggage buyer in a department store, admitted feeling that he was in a bad rut. Bill, on the other hand, was enthusiastic about his work, about his company and its product, and especially about his future in the organization. He showed Jerry a picture of his new house and invited him to bring his wife over for a visit on the following Sunday afternoon.

When the two men resumed their discussion on Sunday, Jerry ventured a tentative inquiry about the possibility of a connection with Bill's company. "As a matter of fact," said Bill, "I've been talking to our sales manager about you. Mr. Clark said he's been thinking of adding a couple of new salesmen and would be glad to have a talk with you."

Since Jerry still had a week's vacation coming to him, it was easy to arrange an appointment with Mr. Clark, who suggested that Jerry might like to spend a few days in the field with his friend Bill "to get the feel of the situation."

At the end of the third day the two men sat down to review some of the things that had occurred. Bill said, "Now that you have watched me making ten or a dozen calls, what do you think of the job? Would you feel happy doing that sort of thing?"

Jerry shook his head. "Never," he declared promptly. "Why not?" asked Bill.

Jerry was a bit embarrassed to explain. "Well, for one thing, when you called on that man Jones this morning, and you found him busy on the telephone, you went right out in the stock room and asked the clerk how many cases of your brand he had left, and then you told Mr. Jones how many you were going to put him down for. When he tried to cut the amount in half, you got him to agree to your figure and told him you would ship half the order now and the other half in 90 days."

"Well, of course," said Bill, "why should I leave the door open for some competitor to get a piece of that business?"

Jerry went on, "And yesterday, when Mr. Allen began by saying he'd rather wait until you saw him next month, you talked him into a trial order on some new item he'd never heard of, and. . . ."

Bill couldn't help laughing. "Seems to me you actually felt sorry for all those people I sold during these three days, Jerry. Was there a single one who seemed unhappy when we shook hands as I left? Did you hear Tom Allen ask how soon he might expect delivery of that new item? Somebody has to take charge in every sales interview, Jerry. And if we make a habit of letting the customer do it, we simply can't call ourselves salesmen. Tell me, how do you do it in your line?"

Jerry said, "Well, let's say we ran an ad in the TIMES for a special sale of cowhide one-suiter cases at $39.75. Suppose that next morning you had the ad in your hand as you stepped off the elevator into our department. I would sell you what you came in for." Bill said, "No, you would just take my order."

Jerry replied defensively, "Well, before writing up the order, I would also show you a two-suiter in the same leather at $47.50. And if you seemed interested, I would call your attention to a new combination bag with an outside zipper compartment at $57.50. In fact, that's just what I did with an old customer two weeks ago."

Bill said, "But in most cases, the prospect would dictate the decision, isn't that so?"

Jerry nodded and thought the matter over before replying, "Yes, my friend, and that's probably why I haven't made more progress in my job. Maybe I should do a little more of this 'taking charge of things' in other phases of my work, too."

When the two men met again six months later, Jerry had some good news for his friend. "We are opening a branch store in that new suburban shopping center in Springtown. And they are making me the manager, chiefly because I walked into the office of the president of the real estate company and told him my company wanted an option on one of their best corner locations. We got in ahead of the competition because I took charge of the situation!"

The hallmark of a successful salesman is the ability to make his prospects do the things they know they should be doing.

What Would You Have Done?

Joe Jenkins was a salesman of convention facilities for a Florida resort hotel. Looking over the guest register one morning, he spotted the name of Kenneth B. Taylor, sales vice president of an important company, who was evidently spending his winter vacation there with his wife.

Introducing himself on the hotel veranda that afternoon, Joe asked Mr. and Mrs. Taylor how they were enjoying their stay. "Perfectly wonderful place," said Mrs. Taylor, "we have a marvelous view from our window, and the service has been superb." Mr. Taylor added, "And your recreational facilities are simply tops."

Joe then inquired, "When do you plan to hold your next company convention?" Mr. Taylor shook his head, "Probably not until the fall of next year, or maybe the following spring."

Jenkins knew the importance of getting a commitment from Taylor before he had a chance to listen to proposals for holding his convention elsewhere. He took a notebook from his pocket and said, "We are booking a great many important conventions for as far as three years ahead. Let me show you some of the . . ."

Mr. Taylor waved the matter aside. "It's much too early to go into that now, Mr. Jenkins. No, you'd better get in touch with me next fall."

Well, if you were in Joe Jenkins' shoes, *What Would You Have Done?*

(*see* page 190)

19

GETTING
THE SIGNATURE
AND DEPOSIT

In our earlier discussion we mentioned the importance of bringing the order blank into play as soon as the prospect indicates serious interest in your proposition. We stated that the more details you can begin to enter on your order pad, the more confident you can be of the buyer's acceptance.

But the inexperienced salesman says, "When do I ask him to sign the order? How do I get his name on the dotted line?"

That Fearsome Dotted Line

Overcredulous people have so often been cheated or defrauded by unscrupulous operators that there is a wide-spread fear of the consequences of "signing on the dotted line." Honest salesmen, therefore, carefully avoid any reference to this fearsome symbol of gullibility.

Many sales, in fact, do not even require the buyer's signature. Business transactions running into millions of dollars are frequently closed by telephone, or even by a nod of the head or a handshake.

However, in order to be legally binding, some form of signed agreement is usually necessary. Even the wealthy realtor who has agreed over the luncheon table to pay $1,000,000 for a hotel or office building eventually affixes his signature to a formal contract of sale. The point is that a definite commitment has been made before he is asked to sign anything.

The Signature Is a Mere Formality

Since most sales are closed by some form of implied consent before the complete details are recorded on paper, the buyer's signature becomes a mere formality to which as little importance should be attached as possible.

Let's assume you are a life insurance salesman. After the commitment has been obtained for a specific kind and amount of insurance and you have completed the answers on the application form, you fill in the date and sign your name as witness. You then hand the form and your pen to the prospect and say, "Just put your name there next to mine." Or you may ask him to "please verify the statements I have written down."

If you are a furniture salesman and have helped Mr. and Mrs. Clarke select a dining room set, you may ask the gentleman, "Do you spell your name with an E?" and "What is your street number again?" And after you have written down his answers, you hand him your pencil and show him where to put his name or his initials.

How to Get the Deposit

Ted Hawkins, a veteran closer of hundreds of sales, says, "All experienced salesmen know the importance of getting a deposit with the order. Each prospect requires particular treatment, and each case presents its own special problem. And this is where too many salesmen fall down. Not because of the problem itself, but because of their *fear* of the problem."

Ted was once asked to address a large group of salesmen on "Closing the Sale." During the question-and-answer period following his talk, a voice from the audience asked, "How do you get the deposit?"

Ted said, "Oh, there's lots of ways. Let's ask some of you people out there on the floor." After allowing a number of volunteers to describe their methods, Ted shook his head. "I'm still waiting for somebody to give us the one best answer." Then, cupping a hand behind his ear, he called to a young chap in the rear of the room, "I believe you have it. A little louder, please." The answer came loud and clear, "ASK FOR IT."

It's the Normal Way

When you or I buy a piano or a fur coat or an automobile, we naturally expect that a down payment of some sort will be required to confirm our purchase. Now that charge accounts and credit cards provide such popular and convenient methods of payment, people find it perfectly normal to bind the transaction by signing their names. So when you ask your customer how he would prefer to pay for his purchase, he does not hesitate to tell you.

Don't Throw the Ball Away

Tommy Burr closed his first five encyclopedia sales by following his training instructions to the letter. Most of these were to people he knew. But then he ran into a string of cancellations, so he came to Mr. Morgan, his manager, for advice.

"Tell me how this began," the manager asked. "I noticed that you took a deposit with each of your first five sales, but not with these last three. What happened with this Murphy case?"

"Well, frankly, I forgot to ask Mrs. Murphy for a deposit, and the next day she telephoned that she and her husband had talked it over and wanted to cancel the order. Then on my next sale, I got both Mr. and Mrs. Frankel to agree on our monthly payment plan, but when I asked for the deposit they wanted to wait until his next pay day. He signed the order all right, but when I came around for the money, his wife said they had changed their minds. So now I make sure to ask the prospect for the money before he signs the order."

Mr. Morgan remained silent for a moment, then reached into his waste basket for the newspaper he had discarded on his arrival at the office. Turning to the sport page, he pointed to the headline, CUBS WIN ON JOHNSON'S ERROR.

Mr. Morgan began reading from the baseball reporter's story:

"With two men out in the ninth inning, Higgins walked the next batter. Denny Doyle, a weak hitter, bounced a grounder to Jim Johnson at short. Jimmy, eager to make the double play, failed to come up with the ball cleanly, then made a hurried throw which landed in deep right field. Both runners scored on the error and the game was over."

Mr. Morgan put the paper aside and said, "That's your trouble, Tom. You are so concerned about getting the money that you are actually throwing the order away. Don't you remember that we taught you in training class: First make sure to get the prospect's firm commitment. Then have him put his O.K. on the order blank. *After* he has done that, and not before, you start to make out a receipt for his deposit as you ask him, 'How much do you want to pay me now?' Don't worry about the double play until you've made sure of the first out."

Tommy Burr has been playing errorless ball ever since.

What Would You Have Done?

Jim Gardner's father was a lawyer. When Jim finished college he took a job selling law books for a Denver publisher in a somewhat scattered territory.

Returning to headquarters after his first successful road trip, Jim was surprised to hear that he had been chosen to address a regional sales conference on "How to Get a Deposit with the Order."

The manager explained, "A lot of our old-timers overlook one of our most important inducements: the company pays the shipping charges on all orders which are accompanied by a cash deposit. When the salesman takes an order without a prepayment, he risks the possibility of a cancellation. And the buyer pays more than he should have. I want you to tell those buzzards how you closed your first 14 sales with cash on the barrel head. What's your secret?" *What Do You Suppose Jim Told Him?*

(*see* page 191)

20

GET OUT

Few things are sadder than losing a sale you have already closed. But it can happen, and often it will, if you make the mistake of lingering after the transaction has been concluded. As one old pro puts it, "Close your mouth when you close the sale!"

Even if your buyer is an established customer or a personal friend, *get out*. This is no time for small talk or polite chatter, and no time to ask for leads. *Get out!*

The untimely arrival of one of the prospect's friends or business associates, who may have other ideas to offer which may change his mind, can destroy all the good work you have done.

So it's better to be on your way. Before leaving, however, be sure to thank the buyer for his courtesy and his confidence. Your final impression should leave a pleasant memory in his mind.

It is not usually necessary to thank him for his business. Often as not, he should be thanking you for what you have done for him, and frequently he will say as much.

If he asks you to stay for a bit of refreshment, tell him you'll be glad to take a rain-check, but you have to keep another appointment.

Say, "It's been a real pleasure to serve you, Mr. Jones." And then, *on your way!*

What Would You Have Done?

Dick Webster, travel agent, had good reason to feel pleased with the result of his call at the home of Mr. and Mrs. Robinson. After a discussion lasting several hours, he had signed them up for an extended European vacation starting in June.

The long interview had ended on a friendly note after a prolonged debate between the Robinsons concerning the comparative merits of joining an organized tour or traveling independently on their own. But finally all the details had been ironed out, the reservation forms signed, and everybody was happy.

Five minutes later, when Dick stopped at the bank nearby to cash a personal check, he discovered that he had forgotten his fountain pen. He recalled loaning it to Mr. Robinson to write out a check for the deposit.

The pen was especially valuable to Dick, having been presented to him upon the completion of his term as president of the American Travel Association.

He was about to go back and pick it up, but . . . Well, *What Would You Have Done?*

(*see* page 191)

21

KEEPING THE SALE CLOSED

Three veteran sales managers were talking one evening about the great salesmen they had known. One declared that the best salesman he had ever met sold farm machinery in Ohio. The second man awarded the palm to an automobile salesman in Worcester, Mass. And the third sang the praises of a building supply salesman in a suburban territory in Pennsylvania.

WHAT MAKES A GREAT SALESMAN?

Perhaps the most striking point on which these three executives agreed was that the top salesman is not always the man who sells the greatest volume for his company. Nor does he necessarily operate in the heart of a great city where there are more potential buyers. Nor is he always the best-educated, best-dressed or most brilliant personality on the sales force.

But year in and year out he produces an above-average volume of sales to an above-average number of repeat customers who give him practically all of their business. This in contrast to the clever prima donna who may achieve sensational results for a brief period, and who then tapers off into mediocrity or disappears from the scene completely, leaving a trail of dissatisfied buyers behind him.

The one common denominator of selling excellence, these expert observers agreed, was the *ability to keep their customers sold.* Not for just one sale, or one season or a year, but as the song says, ALWAYS. Each of their nominees for "The Best Salesman I Ever Knew" possessed that priceless combination of qualities which creates complete customer-loyalty and confidence.

Good Will, the Salesman's Priceless Asset

According to a famous decision of the United States Supreme Court, "Good will is the inclination of the buyer to return to the source of earlier satisfaction." Big corporations, when acquiring ownership of another company, have been known to pay as much as a million dollars for good will, which is the favorable reputation enjoyed by the company and its product.

The successful salesman can place a similar cash value on his *personal good will.* But unlike the good will of a company, which can be purchased by another, the individual salesman's personal good will is non-transferable.

It Must Be Earned

A long-established automobile dealer has successfully represented three different makes of cars over a 27 year period. He says, "I can take the poorest automobile made, give superior service, and build a successful business. Or I can take the best auto made, give poor service, and go broke."

The best rule of conduct remains the Golden Rule, "doing unto others as you would have them do unto you." But the top salesman does not stop there. He tries to do *more* for the other fellow than he would expect in return.

Make Good on Your Promises

The most overworked word in the vocabulary of business is *service.* Some salesmen become so careless in their extravagant assurances of future service that they experience difficulty in living up to their promises.

Nothing will destroy the buyer's confidence so quickly as the discovery, or even the suspicion, that the salesman is promising more than he can possibly deliver. On the other hand, nothing is so certain to win the customer's permanent good will as the salesman's faithful performance of every promise he has made.

Sewing Up the After-Sale

Too many salesmen, unfortunately, are more intent on closing the sale than on buttoning up the after-sale. They forget that the buyer is much more concerned about what happens *after* he buys than before. And that this will determine whether he will want to buy from him again.

A North Carolina insurance salesman, when delivering a policy to a new client, says, "I want you to know, Mr. Jones, that I don't consider this to be the *end* of something, but really the *beginning* of something. I'm never going to forget the responsibility I assumed when you chose me as your insurance man. I hope to deserve the confidence you have placed in me."

It is no wonder that this man's sales volume ranks among the highest and his lapsation record among the lowest of all the salesmen in his company. He keeps his sales closed by remembering the poet's phrase, "For I have promises to keep."

Don't Destroy Your Employer's Good Will

A company may have established a national reputation for a good product backed up by superior service. But a poor salesman can tear down his employer's favorable image by failing to live up to the company's high standards in his personal performance.

John Stanton had always driven one make of automobile, having bought three successive cars from a dealer who had given him exceptionally good service.

Now that he had moved to another city, he walked into the showroom of the local dealer and selected one of the new models. But something about the salesman who took his order made him remark, "I think I should tell you that I have been somewhat spoiled by the man from whom I have bought my cars in the past. The real reason for my purchase this morning is that Joe Taylor had a reputation for outstanding service in our town, and that's why so many people wouldn't think of buying any other car."

The salesman smiled expansively as he drew a card from his pocket and presented it to the customer, "My name is George S. Jones, and Service is my middle name. In fact, if there's one thing our company insists upon it's good service. You see, according to our rule book I am required to keep in touch with each of my customers at least once every 90 days. You'll be hearing from me, don't worry."

Three months later Mr. Stanton's secretary told him, "A Mr. Jones telephoned while you were out. He said you could call him back if you had any complaints about your car."

Another 90 days passed. This time Mr. Stanton answered the phone himself when Jones called. "Hello there, this is George Jones. I thought I'd call up to find out how the old bus is behaving. Having any trouble?"

Mr. Stanton managed to maintain his composure as he replied, "I don't like your calling my new car an old bus. As it happens, my wife and I are quite delighted with it. In fact, her brother has bought one just like it on the strength of our good report. And my business partner likes it so well he is trading in his two year old car for one like ours in a larger model. . . ."

Salesman Jones interrupted, "But why didn't you let me know? I'd have been glad to take care of them."

Mr. Stanton explained, "That's just the point. You seem to think that taking care of a customer means nothing more than selling him a car. Perhaps you should read your company's rule book a little more carefully."

The Automatic Prospector

George Jones' poor performance points up another important difference between the top salesman and the mediocre man. The unsuccessful fellow keeps complaining about his lack of prospects and the failure of his customers to "tip him off" when friends or relatives express approval of their purchase.

The top man cultivates the good will of his satisfied customers so that they become an almost automatic source of new prospects. He takes every opportunity to contact them in person, both to head off possible complaints and to expose himself to their friends, neighbors and business associates.

Ted Jackson is such a man. In fact, he says, he has more prospects than he can find time to follow up.

GETTING CARDS AND LETTERS OF INTRODUCTION

Ted is especially successful in obtaining cards of introduction from his clients. He explained his method to an associate who confessed his inability to get such cooperation from his customers:

> In the first place, I make an all-out effort to give my buyer the best service he's ever had, better than he really expects. Very often he will tell me exactly that. This gives me an opportunity to ask him about some specific person I want to meet. I may say, "The other day you spoke of your lawyer, Jim Clarke." Or I may ask, "Who is that man who left your office as I came in? Seems to me I've seen him before." Or I may ask about his partner, or his neighbor or his brother-in-law. Then I tell him I have been wanting to make this man's acquaintance. We talk about him for a bit, possibly about his business, family or social connection.
>
> And then I suggest, "If Mr. Blank came in that door right now, you wouldn't hesitate to introduce me, would you?" He promptly agrees, of course. So I hand him a card, already filled out with my name and a space for his signature, and I say to him, "Then I'm sure you won't mind signing this card for me." Almost never do I meet with a refusal. Frequently my customer will prefer to dictate his own letter of introduction. And the other day a fellow who felt he should have given me a larger order did even better than that. He called up a couple of his friends and said he wanted them to meet the two of us for lunch at his club.

Ted says he learned an important lesson by watching the champions play golf and billiards: "They play every shot so that the ball is in position for the next shot. I try to have each of my sales put me in position for the next sale."

Or, as a top man in the office appliance field puts it, "The delivery is the final step in the first sale, and the first step in the next sale."

"What
Would You
Have Done?"

(Answers)

1. PREPARING THE GROUND FOR THE INTERVIEW

Fred asked, "Have you ever met his secretary?"

John answered, "I've talked with her on the telephone. Miss Harper has always been very pleasant. Seems like a nice person."

"Then why don't you try to see her when Mr. Dusenbury is out to lunch or at a meeting? You may pick up some helpful information."

Following Fred's advice, John called at the company's headquarters during the noon hour next day. Greeting the receptionist with a smile, he said, "Please tell Miss Harper Mr. Underwood would like to speak to her."

As she approached from the private office, John handed her his card and said, "Good afternoon, Miss Harper."

She replied pleasantly, "Oh, you're the gentleman who has been trying to make an appointment with Mr. Dusenbury. I'm so sorry, but he just left for an important luncheon meeting."

John answered, "That's just fine, because I wanted to talk to you instead. I appreciate how impossible it has been to squeeze an appointment for me into Mr. Dusenbury's busy calender. But I've been wondering. Isn't there some odd hour, maybe the early morning or late afternoon, when he might spare a few minutes to discuss the subject I've written on the back of that card?"

Miss Harper turned the card, and apparently recognized the name of the mining company. "Well, there could just be a possibility. You might do this. I usually arrive here around 9 o'clock in the morning, but Mr. Dusenbury gets here quite a bit earlier. His

169

apartment is just a short walk from the office, and he likes to get an early start before the telephone starts ringing."

The rest was easy. Miss Harper attached John's card to a memorandum she placed on Mr. Dusenbury's desk before she left that evening: "This gentleman wondered whether you would be interested in talking with him about the XYZ Mining Company. He may drop in early tomorrow morning."

Next day John was at the Dusenbury office before 8:15. Nobody was in sight, but he could hear papers being shuffled in the president's office. John coughed, and Mr. Dusenbury came to the door with the memo and John's card in his hand. "Does your name happen to be Underwood?" he asked with a smile.

John nodded and was invited to step in. Twenty minutes later he left with a firm offer to buy the block of XYZ Mining Company stock.

Picking the right time and place for the interview had made the sale possible.

2. GET OFF ON THE RIGHT FOOT

Lew withdrew to the farther side of the room to examine some framed photographs on the wall.

Mr. Gilman remarked, as he hung up the phone, "Sorry you happened to catch me on such a busy day." But Lew was apparently too absorbed in the pictures to notice what he said. Then he burst out excitedly, "Where in the world did you get that fine catch of small mouth bass? What sort of tackle did you use? And you sure had the right light for that camera shot!"

Mr. Gilman promptly forgot about his busy work schedule. "So you're a fisherman, too! I don't think anybody ever noticed those pictures before. I like to keep them handy to remind me there's something else to do besides spinning the grindstone."

Lew Cochran, having uncovered his prospect's pet hobby, followed up with a trump card. "The trout season opens next week. Let's you and I get together early Thursday morning and drive up to Rondout Creek. I've got a nice new sports model just waiting for this kind of an outing. What do you say?"

Mr. Gilman's capitulation was complete. Several weeks later he remarked to Miss Jepson, "It's a funny thing. If you had told me a month ago that I would be going fishing on a cold April morning, and that I would end up owning a new sports car, and that I would invite the man who sold it to me to spend a weekend with us at Southampton next summer, I'd have said you were out of your mind!"

Yes, one of the best ways to get off on the right foot is to hook up with your prospect's hobby.

3. Building Personal Prestige

This is how George Evanson set about transferring his personal prestige from St. Louis to New York.

He called on each of his 50 best policy owners in St. Louis. After a friendly discussion of his client's business he inquired, "Who is your best friend (or customer, or supplier) in New York City?"

If his client said John Jones, he would ask when he had seen him last, did he seem in good health, and was his business prospering?

He then explained that for personal reasons he had decided to transfer his life insurance business to New York—"and frankly, I've been wondering how I'm going to make a fresh start in building a clientele. This man Jones sounds like the sort of man I would like to meet. Would you mind letting me have a letter of introduction? Perhaps you would like to mention that I've been handling your life insurance, and that you think I might be able to render a valuable service to him. . . ."

By the time George had set up his new office in the Empire State, he had accumulated nearly a hundred letters to leading New York business executives from their friends in the west, each recommending Mr. Evanson in the highest terms. And during his first year in New York, he qualified as usual for his annual membership in the Million Dollar Round Table.

4. SALES TOOLS AND EQUIPMENT

With two or three competitors trying to top each other's claims for their respective oil burners, Fred recognized the necessity of recalling the superior advantages of gas heating to the attention of his prospects.

He selected an attractive reprint of a recent magazine advertisement, which stressed in separate paragraphs such headlined features as

Cleanliness
No Moving Parts
Silence of Operation
Instantaneous Hot Water
No Worry About Fuel Deliveries

Since Mrs. Wilson had mentioned the difficulty of obtaining an emergency supply of pea coal for their old coal furnace last winter, Fred circled the paragraph about Fuel Deliveries in red crayon and wrote in the margin, "This is the point we were discussing when you called."

He enclosed the reprint in a letter addressed to Mr. and Mrs. Wilson, in which he quoted the comment of a gas furnace user in their neighborhood: "Last fall you gave us an estimate of $250 for one year's consumption of gas in our new heating equipment. We are happy to report that our gas bills for twelve months came to only $229."

Then Fred added a footnote: "Our display room is open on Monday evenings. I hope I may see you between 8 and 9 next Monday, the 23rd. F. D. Bates."

Next morning he received a phone call from Mr. Wilson. "Thanks for helping us make up our minds about that gas furnace. I'd like to come over right away and settle the matter so we can shut off any more sales talks about oil burners."

Your company's advertising can help you close sales, if you give it a chance.

5. QUALIFY THE PROSPECT— MAKE HIM TALK

Jim was flustered, and he showed it. Later on, when he had a chance to think the matter over, he felt that he might have countered Mr. Pickering's question by asking lightheartedly whether he had any attractive leases or deeds of trust for sale.

But Mr. Pickering proceeded to add to his young caller's discomfiture by asking, "How is Mr. Roundtree these days? Haven't seen him at the club for some time."

Jim managed an awkward smile. "Oh, he's fine, I understand. I haven't seen him since he returned from Europe last week. I wasn't aware that you knew him. Frankly, I came in to inquire whether you would be interested in subscribing to our weekly journal."

Mr. Pickering seemed surprised. "Evidently you don't read your journal as carefully as some people. It contained one of my articles a few weeks ago, and I have been getting a number of inquiries for additional information. I don't have time to read the magazine here at the office, so I've had it mailed to my home in Scarsdale for many years."

Poor Jim. He made one more gallant

attempt. "Have you heard of our new edition of the New York Inheritance Tax Statutes? Two of your neighbors here in the building placed orders with me just this morning."

Mr. Pickering remained in charge of the discussion. "Yes, this is the third time my partner, John Waldron, has had his name on the title page as one of the collaborators. He has just received a set from Mr. Roundtree in appreciation of his work on this revised edition."

By this time Jim was wondering how he could escape without further embarrassment.

Mr. Pickering held out his hand sympathetically. "I know you haven't enjoyed your visit here this morning. And neither have I, for that matter. Because I recall one or two situations from my early youth as a bond salesman. One of my prospects taught me a lesson I never forgot. I had plunged into an enthusiastic sales talk about some railroad bonds I wanted him to buy. He sat there listening quietly, waiting for me to stop talking. When I finally gave him a chance to say a word, he explained that he had been a director of the road for 20 years and had voted in favor of the bond issue only a few weeks before."

Mr. Pickering concluded with this piece of advice: "Always qualify your prospect in advance. Try to make him do the talking. And never jump to conclusions. The one you jump to may be your own!"

6. The Salesman's Attitude

Sam Brown was embarrassed to have been chosen to relate his experience to so many older men in the business.

"I didn't realize I was doing anything different with these leads than anybody else. Maybe it's because of what happened on the first advertising lead I ever got. The coupon was signed with an ordinary name like W. H.

Green. The address was in the suburban town where I live. I called there one morning, found it was an apartment house, and one of the first floor letter boxes had the name Robert F. Green. Nobody answered the bell, so I decided to try again that evening.

"Since this was my first lead, I did a lot of thinking before I went back. Evidently this was a married couple, both working, and the wife had probably seen our ad in one of the women's magazines, probably *American Home*. Maybe they were planning to move. Perhaps they had seen a house they liked, but it needed a lot of repairs. Our ad showed pictures of people making their own alterations, and the coupon offered a booklet with complete information.

"I figured the wife had read the booklet, maybe showed it to her husband. It was interesting, but it didn't give them *the information they wanted*—the one thing everybody wants to know: *What does it cost?*"

Sam went on. "As I drove over to their place that evening I said to myself, 'These people went to a lot of trouble to get information about our product. The headline of our ad interrupted their reading of a magazine. They read the whole page, including the coupon. They clipped it, found an envelope, addressed it and stamped it and made sure to mail it. And when the booklet came, they still didn't have *the information they wanted.*'

"When I got to the apartment, a young couple had just locked the door on their way out, probably on the way to dinner. I asked them, 'Are you Mr. and Mrs. Green?' They nodded, so I introduced myself, 'My name's Brown, with the Apex Insulation Company. My company sent you a booklet recently, but it probably didn't give you the information you wanted. We couldn't quote prices, for example, without knowing which of our products would be best for your particular purpose. I live only a few blocks away, so I'll be glad to come over some evening and give you *all the information*

helpful

you want. How about 7:30 tomorrow evening?'

"They looked at each other, smiled back at me, and the husband said, 'All right, better make it 8 o'clock. I've got a lot of questions to ask you.'"

Sam concluded, "I made three sales in the next couple of months as the result of that one lead. So my attitude with every advertising lead is always the same: This person *still wants the information* which he didn't find in the booklet, and I'm going to see that he gets it."

7. SINCERITY AND CONVICTION

Sid had been hearing the same kind of story from Dr. Graham for a long time: "Not now, perhaps after Election Day, maybe collections will be better by then," and so on. Sid sincerely liked the doctor and couldn't help feeling a bit sorry for him. He had heard some of his patients speak highly of his professional skill and his unusual patience with children and nervous old ladies.

But with his office tucked away in a side street that had been part of a fashionable neighborhood in his uncle's day, he could scarcely hope to expand his practice in competition with his more up-to-date brethren.

So Sid decided on an unusual approach. He knew the doctor made no appointments for Wednesday afternoons, reserving that time for his personal affairs and occasional recreation. Sid called him on the telephone, "I have been wanting to talk to you, doctor, about a matter of great importance. It's something that concerns you very seriously. Will you have lunch with me on Wednesday?"

The doctor seemed surprised, but after a moment's thought he agreed, "Let's make it for lunch at my club. If you meet me there around 12:30 we can spend a leisurely hour together before I meet Mrs. Graham for a shopping trip."

At the luncheon table on Wednesday, Dr. Graham came right to the point. "What is this important thing you wanted to tell me?"

Sid took a card from his pocket and laid it face down beside his plate. Then he asked, "When does your lease expire, doctor?"

"Next fall, in October; why do you ask?"

"Suppose that I told you that you couldn't renew your lease, that the building was being sold and you would have to get out."

The doctor looked worried, "Where did you hear that?"

"Well, it isn't official, but I understand the state university is looking into the possibility of opening a new campus somewhere in that neighborhood. But let's assume it's true. You would have to move, isn't that so?"

"Well, yes. But I'd have to look around."

Sid continued, "Of course, but the fact is you *would* relocate your office. And regardless of the political situation, or a possible stock market recession, or any other temporary condition, people would still be getting sick and your services would be in demand. And so you would decide to move." The doctor nodded.

"Then why don't you decide right now? You're not yet 40, and with more than 20 years of active practice ahead of you, you certainly aren't going to stay in that hole-in-the-wall forever, are you?"

The doctor smiled. "Thank you, I'm 42. But you are right about not getting many new patients to replace those that move away. Have you any specific suggestions?"

Sid picked up the card and passed it across the table. Dr. Graham turned it over and read the typewritten message, "He who must see everything clearly before he decides, never decides."

Sid explained, "My father had that motto framed and hung on the wall of his office. He taught all of us that successful people don't wait until decisions are forced upon them. They anticipate them."

Dr. Graham took a long time before replying. "Funny thing, but Grace and I have talked about this many times . . . when we got married . . . when we bought our first car . . . when we bought our home. She was always the one to anticipate the future and insist it would all work out. And it always has, somehow."

The doctor slapped the table. "All right, my friend, many thanks for your sincere advice. I'm going to tell Grace this afternoon that I'm moving my office this summer. And I don't think she will try to talk me out of it."

Two weeks later Sid Saunders received a telephone call from Mrs. Graham. "I wanted you to be the first to know that the doctor has signed up for a ten year lease in that new professional building in the heart of town. He will be wanting to talk to you about the equipment. But first I wanted to thank you, oh so very much, for getting him out of that dreadful rut!"

8. Close Early and Often

Mr. Walker quietly replied, "You're right, John. I didn't hear any of the conversation upstairs. But all I heard down here was your 'good-bye' instead of some comment like, 'I'll call you this evening to let you know how I make out,' or 'Just mail your deposit to me,' while handing them your card."

"I couldn't have said anything like that to these people. You don't know what you're talking about."

The manager nodded. "Maybe you're right, John, but I've been watching your tactics for some time. I just can't remember the last time you asked a prospect to buy. I'll tell you what. The next time a prospect asks for a spinet, tell them Mr. Walker takes care of that department, and let me go upstairs with you. I may not close the sale, but it won't be because I didn't give the prospect a good chance to buy."

Later in the afternoon a couple asked John about spinet models. He beckoned to Mr. Walker, "Would you mind showing these people a spinet?"

On the way up in the elevator Mr. Walker quietly asked, "Do you live in town?" The husband answered, "No, we have an apartment in Larchmont."

Arriving on the second floor, Mr. Walker began by asking, "Do either of you play the piano?" The lady replied, "No, this is for our daughter. Nancy is having her ninth birthday next week and we've promised her a piano."

Since they had not brought the little girl with them, Mr. Walker guessed correctly that she had not begun to take lessons. Also, since neither of the parents played themselves, they would probably be less interested in the tonal qualities of the instrument than its appearance, and probably price.

He took them to a group of spinet pianos which were arranged in an alcove. "Here we have several different shades of walnut and mahogany, and this one is an especially attractive model in maple. Would you want to place your piano in the living room?"

Mr. Taylor answered, "Since Nancy has a good-sized room of her own, I thought we might put it there. I noticed downstairs you had a larger piano on display in some sort of light wood, which would come closer to matching Nancy's other pieces. What is that called?"

"That's a blond finished walnut. In fact, I can quote you an attractive price on that. Let me show it to you."

Mr. Taylor quickly spoke up. "I saw that as we came in. But it's much too big. What are the prices on some of these?"

"This one is $575. Here's the same instrument in a different finish, $625. Do you like it?" Mrs. Taylor looked at her husband who said, "We saw an ad of a spinet model in yesterday's paper at $450."

"There it is," said Mr. Walker, pointing to a very plain instrument against the wall, "the same one that Casey's department store is featuring at $450. Let me play it for you."

Mr. Walker sat down and ran his fingers up and down the keys, ending up with the opening bars of Chopin's "Polonaise." Then he did the same on one of the pianos in the group they had looked at before. Even an amateur could notice the marked difference in the quality of the two instruments. "Which do you like better?" he asked Mrs. Taylor.

"This one sounds very much better," she admitted, "but we didn't want to spend over $500."

"In that case I can do something for you," said Mr. Walker, getting out his order blank. "Where do you live in Larchmont? . . . Clearview Gardens?" He wrote it down and asked for the apartment number. Then, as he copied the model number from the tag on the maple piano, he continued, "I have a good customer in Larchmont, a Mrs. Franklin Henderson. She is a well known musician and she sends us quite a few people. She may be able to recommend a good teacher for your daughter."

He went on, "As you see, this piano in maple is priced at $550. Do you have an old piano which we can credit against the new one? No? Well, the least we could offer you for any trade-in would be $50. And of course, you will need to have a bench, which would cost $50 in maple to match the piano. So I'm going to ask Mr. Harmon to let you have this piano and the bench together for $550. I can't be sure, of course, but if you give me a small deposit this afternoon I'll telephone you tomorrow how I make out with Mr. Harmon."

On the telephone next morning, Mr. Taylor had only one question, "Could we arrange for monthly payments?"

9. Always Talk About YOU

Following his usual custom, Joe Jordan decided that he would make no attempt to contact Mr. Barton until he had obtained some information about him. He found that the hotel was not far from Carnegie Hall and that it was patronized by concert singers and other leading figures in the musical world.

When he asked for Mr. Henry Barton at the desk, the clerk did not recognize the name. But then he volunteered, "Perhaps you are looking for Mr. Bartonelli, the operatic tenor. He usually stays with us when he is in New York."

Joe recalled hearing about Lawrence Tibbett, whose Italian voice teacher had tried without success to persuade him to change his professional name to Lorenzo Tibbetto. And so it seemed a good guess that Henry Barton and Enrico Bartonelli were the same person!

When Joe asked the desk clerk whether he knew anything about Mr. Bartonelli's current whereabouts, he replied, "Yes, we understand that he is going to sing on that All Star Concert which will be broadcast from the Hollywood Bowl next Sunday evening."

Although Joe did not pretend to know very much about "long hair music", he and his wife made sure to listen to the broadcast on Sunday, when Mr. Bartonelli received an ovation for his expert rendition of three operatic numbers.

Having learned from the clerk that Mr. Bartonelli had reserved his usual suite for the following month, Joe made it his business to drop in at the hotel for Sunday Brunch a few weeks later. By good fortune he recognized Mr. Bartonelli from his photograph, seated alone at a nearby table. As the two gentlemen left the dining room together, Joe ventured a pleasant smile which the singer returned.

As they entered the lobby, Joe spoke up. "I beg your pardon, but aren't you Signor Bartonelli? My wife and I heard you sing on that broadcast the other night, and we agreed that neither of us had ever heard such a magnificent rendition of the Paggliacci 'Prologue.' "

Mr. B. was delighted, and after a brief conversation he invited Joe to come up to his suite. Over a social drink he inquired, "What is your business, Mr. Jordan? Are you a musician?"

Joe explained, "No, I'm in the investment business. Frankly, my wife is the musician of the family. She plays the piano and attends the opera quite regularly. I don't often find the time."

A little later Mr. Bartonelli became quite confidential. "You mentioned being in the investment business. As you probably know, professional singers are notoriously incompetent in handling their financial affairs. A few weeks ago I was reading an advertisement about Mutual Funds. What do you know about them?"

Joe was happy for the opportunity to educate his new-found prospect. When he left the apartment a couple of hours later, he tucked a pair of complimentary tickets for Signor Bartonelli's next concert in his pocket.

Joe turned to thank his new client, who answered, "The pleasure has been mine, Joe. And next time, please call me Henry!"

10. Make it Hard to Get—Easy to Buy

A few days later Brad Benson received a telephone call from his friend Jack. "You and I are teamed up again for the Scotch foursome at next Friday's golf outing. Let me pick you up around 9:30. Okay? See you then."

On Friday morning Brad was surprised to see his friend drive up in a white Cadillac. Jack called to him as he unlocked the big trunk, "Throw your clubs and things in here with mine. Sorry I'm late, but this baby will get us there in plenty of time."

"What's the big idea?" said Brad. "Since when are Buick dealers driving Caddies?"

"It's quite a story. Hop in. I'll tell you on the way over." As Jack resumed his place behind the wheel, Brad leaned over to read the mileage on the speedometer—a little over 4,000 miles. "Whose car is this?" he asked.

Jack said, "I don't know whether you knew Bruce Bellinger, the president of National Staples. He lived in Centerville." Brad remembered the name, but didn't know he was president of the company.

Jack continued, "He was elected president last December. First thing he did was to buy this new Cadillac and take his wife to Florida for a winter vacation. A week after they got back he died of a heart attack. Mrs. Bellinger never liked to drive a big car so it's been sitting in the garage for four months, while she's been using taxis for her shopping trips."

Brad began to show some interest. Jack went on, "I met her brother Joe in the drug store the other day. He used to work for me, and I asked him whether I might interest his sister in a Buick. He told me she has been looking at cars, so I drove over next morning in one of our smaller jobs in a conservative black model. She liked it a lot. The only problem is the trade-in. I persuaded her to let me borrow the Caddy for today so I could appraise it. It's in wonderful shape, practically brand new. I don't suppose you'd be interested in helping me swing a deal, would you? She's a shrewd customer, and it isn't going to be easy."

Brad didn't say a word until they reached the club. "Let me phone Grace before she goes out. I'll join you later."

Brad called his wife, "Just listen to this. I've got the chance of a lifetime to buy a handsome Cadillac car, practically brand new. . . ."

Ten minutes later Brad told Jack, "I think you've made a deal, Mister. And do you know something? I just took another look at the car, and it's got my monogram, BB, on the door!"

11. How to Start the Order Blank

Since Marjorie and her mother had already rejected a variety of over-fancy patterns during their visits to other stores, Miss Dalrymple was able to concentrate their attention on three or four classic designs. Two of these were finally eliminated, leaving one which Marjorie seemed to like and another which her mother preferred.

The saleslady then turned to Marjorie and said, "You don't have to make your final decision today. Let me show you something."

Miss Dalrymple disappeared for a few minutes. When she returned she laid a separate velvet cloth on the showcase. Then she placed on it a cake knife in the Doric pattern, the one for which Marjorie had indicated her preference.

"Now this is what I suggest you do," said Miss Dalrymple. "Let me send this piece home for you. When you look at it there, away from all these others that seem to confuse you, I'm sure you will like it more than ever. And I know your friends will be very happy with your choice. Of course, if you should decide on some other design in a few days, we can replace this with your new selection."

Miss Dalrymple had already placed her order pad on the counter. "Do you have a charge account?" she asked.

"Yes, but I think I would like to take this with me. I think it's the handsomest silver design I've ever seen. Thank you so much for helping me."

12. Objections—or Mere Excuses?

George Duncan spoke up.

"I like to play the ball game with those fellows. I remember calling on a dealer who was stocking three other lines of appliances. I suggested that he take on just one of our popular items, a portable radio, which would require very little display space.

"His reaction was, 'We carry the XYZ, the best portable radio on the market.'

"I threw the ball back at him, 'Why do you call it the best?'

"He said, 'Well, they were the first to introduce the small transistor model.' So I bounced it back, 'Maybe they brought it out too soon. We waited until we were sure we had knocked all the bugs out of our early experimental sets. Let me show you our latest improvements.'

"He tried another tack, 'They give us the best deal,' so I bounced that one back. 'That's because you stock their whole line instead of a single item.'

"Then he changed his tune by saying he didn't like our company. Naturally I asked him why. When he said he had an unpleasant experience with our credit department some years ago, I knew it was just an excuse. I tried to be tactful by admitting these things sometimes happen, but explained that Jim Breedon, our new credit manager, had been a successful dealer himself for ten years and had a thorough understanding of today's problems.

"He made one more try by saying our line wasn't as well known as the others he carried. I got out my advertising portfolio and knocked the ball over the fence. I told him, 'This full page ad in color, announcing our new portable transistor model, will run in the three top national magazines next month, and people will be walking in your door to ask about it.'

"He let me put him down for two dozen as a starter, and wired a repeat order for five dozen more. He moved into larger quarters last winter, and now he carries our full line.

"Just keep bouncing the ball back to those fellows by asking *why*, *how*, *where* they can do better, and they will provide plenty of openings for you to change their minds."

13. SUPPLY ADDITIONAL REASONS

Ralph hesitated before replying. Then he asked Ben Blake, "Have any of your agents been complaining, either about the cost or the blotters themselves?"

"No, they haven't," Blake admitted, "but I know they will be just as enthusiastic about this new item as they were when we first introduced the calendar blotter idea ten years ago."

Ralph said, "I've been buying my insurance from one of your agents for some time. I remember his telling me last year that he had landed one new account, as the result of this blotter advertising, which would pay his subscription cost for the next five years. I wonder whether there aren't a lot of other fellows who feel the same way. Let's find out."

Ralph then suggested that, inasmuch as he had the names and addresses of over 500 agents whose personal imprints appeared on the monthly blotters, it would be a simple matter to address a letter to each of these men, asking for their confidential opinion of the blotters and whether they felt they should be continued or replaced with something new. "I'll prepare the letters for your signature, Mr. Blake, and we will enclose a stamped return envelope addressed to you personally. I'm willing to abide by whatever the voters decide."

The result was overwhelmingly in favor of continuing the calendar blotters. Many of the men related instances of important new accounts they could trace to the monthly mailings. Several volunteered the statement that if the company should decide to eliminate its participation, they would like to continue the series on a direct basis.

One man wrote, "I have a lawyer-client who complained that his wife always appropriated the blotter I sent to his home, so wouldn't I please send him an extra one to the office. And a few months later his partner telephoned me to inquire how much insurance he would have to buy in order to get on my blotter mailing list."

* * *

Ralph Owens' experience suggests that established customers, as well as new prospects, sometimes need to be given additional reasons for appreciating the salesman's product or service.

14. Enthusiasm

Several years later George Maynard spent his winter vacation in Florida. One of his fishing companions, Frank Downing, turned out to be a retired banker from Clarksville, Mass. When Downing learned that Maynard was vice president of the nationally known beverage company, he inquired, "Would you happen to know about Anthony Fontana? He has the bottling franchise for your brand in our county."

"Yes, I was the man who granted that franchise to Tony Fontana after I had met him just twice. How long have you known him?"

Mr. Downing smiled. "I've known Tony ever since he went to high school and helped his father at the grocery store. He was an enthusiastic youngster, a great booster for all the school teams. He was too small to play football, but he was goalie for the hockey team where he was a holy terror. He pepped up the whole team so they won the state championship three years in a row."

Mr. Maynard nodded, "Sounds just like the young man who came to see me shortly after Fred Fowler died. He told me about his father's grocery business, and how he moved it to a better location and how he expanded their bottled beverage business. And how he always managed to push our brand by seeing that it was available at school rallies, church suppers, firemen's picnics and so on. I remember I was surprised that he mentioned the hockey games too, because most people don't think folks go for cold drinks in the winter."

The banker said, "That was Tony all over. He came to me after his first talk with you people. The bank agreed to back him if he got the franchise, and we were mighty glad he landed it. I guess you are, too."

"Yes, he's got more genuine enthusiasm for our brand than any two other distributors we have. By the way, what's Jerry Fowler doing these days?"

"Oh, he's taking life easy as usual. Lives at his father's old place, spends a lot of time playing golf, hoping to make contacts for his real estate business. If he had one tenth of Tony's enthusiasm he might have amounted to something."

15. MOTIVATION

Janet had a sudden inspiration. "Why not ask Aunt Belle to come out from town for the month of July? She hates to spend the summer in that stuffy apartment and she always loved it here when the children were small. She would take good care of the place, and if somebody came to look at it she could show them around."

Aunt Belle was delighted, especially when Janet suggested she might like to invite some of her friends for bridge or an overnight visit.

Two days after Jim and Janet left on their trip, Aunt Belle invited three of her friends in town to come out on Friday afternoon for bridge. "And we'll have tea on the porch. Let's hope it's a nice day."

On Friday morning Mrs. Hudson telephoned that she couldn't come, but that her daughter-in-law would be glad to take her place. Aunt Belle remembered meeting the younger Mrs. Hudson and her little boy, Billy, so she suggested that she bring him along. "He can watch television while we're playing. And tell him there will be a nice chocolate cake and plenty of Cokes just for him."

Friday turned out a fine sunny day. Aunt Belle's guests came early. She took pride in showing them around the house, with a special story for each room: the convenient nursery, the newly painted bathrooms, the beautiful view from the north bedroom, the spacious kitchen and the big living room where "the Christmas tree always looks so beautiful in that corner." Then she took Billy by the hand and led him outdoors. "I've got something special to show you. Do you see that tree house that Uncle Jim built for Johnny and Helen? Every spring they could watch the mother birds feeding the little ones. What fun they always had!"

As Aunt Belle's guests prepared to leave, Mrs. Hudson called her aside. "This is a wonderful place for raising a family. Billy is asking why we can't have a house like this. I don't suppose your niece would be interested in selling it, would she?"

When Janet telephoned from Halifax on Sunday evening, Aunt Belle told her, "I think I have a buyer for your house. I told them the price you are asking, but they wondered whether you would come down $1,000 because you won't have to pay a broker. . . . You say it's okay? . . . Fine, Mr. Hudson said he would bring me a check for the deposit tomorrow."

As was said before, a good presentation includes both reason and emotion.

16. Implied Consent

Ralph knew that the best offer Mrs. Atwater had received was $31,000. So he felt confident she would accept a firm offer of $37,-000. In any case, it was worth a try.

He reached into a drawer for a printed offering blank. He filled in the figure $37,000 and handed it to Mr. Howard with his pen. "I'll take your signed offer to the owner this afternoon, together with my assurance that she's fortunate to find a purchaser who will be proud to keep the place in as fine a condition as she has always done."

Mrs. Howard smiled at her husband and nodded to him to sign. As he did so he asked, "Would a $500 deposit be satisfactory?"

17. CLOSING ON A MINOR POINT

The salesman realizes that his prospect had planned to buy something less expensive. But he knows the lady will be pleased to own the Japanese Holly, and may even come back for another.

So he brings up a minor point. "Would you want us to deliver and plant it, or will you plant it yourself?" The husband asks, "How much difference in the price?"

The salesman answers, "$35 if we plant it for you, or $27.50 if you take it along and plant it yourself." Mrs. Brown says, "Oh, we'll plant it ourselves."

And the following weekend, she comes back for a second one to match it.

18. TAKE COMMAND

Joe decided to take command of the situation right there.

He looked Kenneth Taylor squarely in the eye and said with a smile, "Speaking from long experience in handling a great many conventions, I can tell you this in all sincerity, Mr. Taylor. Either you will be making this important decision too early, or too late. Which is it going to be?"

Mr. Taylor said nothing, but remained in deep thought.

After several minutes Joe ventured another comment. "You have been very kind in telling me how much you and Mrs. Taylor have enjoyed our service and our facilities this past week. It will be a memorable experience for your associates and employees to meet here in these beautiful surroundings. They will be grateful for your having . . ."

Mr. Taylor broke in: "Yes, you're right, Mr. Jenkins. I can't think of any place that would match this for our purpose. But I've been thinking about something else. I liked what you said about making this important decision too early or too late. That's a wonderful phrase our salesmen could use when they are trying to close a tough sale. We might even make it the theme of our sales convention!"

19. Getting the Signature and Deposit

Jim seemed a little puzzled. Then he said, "After they sign the order, I simply ask them how much deposit they want to give me. If they hesitate, I explain about the shipping charges, and that we will refund their money if not completely satisfied. They just seem to believe me. Frankly, Mr. Johnson, I didn't know we could take orders any other way."

20. Get Out

Dick remembered a somewhat similar experience which had cost his partner, Bill Stone, a substantial commission. Bill had concluded a contract with two couples for a round-the-world cruise, starting from London in the fall, after the two gentlemen retired from their respective businesses.

Shortly after leaving with the signed agreements, Bill found that he had left his portfolio of travel folders and hotel literature behind. So he went back to pick it up—and ran smack into a cancellation.

It appeared that one of the wives, not wanting to start an argument while the travel agent was still there, had quietly gone along with the others until Bill was safely out of the way.

Now that he re-appeared at the door, he was immediately asked to act as umpire in a dispute which had arisen between Mrs. Jones and the three other members of the group.

Mr. Jones explained, "My wife has an overwhelming fear of traveling by air. She keeps referring to that accident when 60 people were killed on their way to France last spring, so she insists we'll have to travel to England by steamer instead of by plane."

Mr. Clark picked up the conversation. "That means we would have to leave almost a week earlier, and that is quite impossible because I am conducting an important meeting on the day before our original departure date." Mrs. Clark chimed in that it was all so silly, and poor Bill never did have a chance to calm down the badly ruffled feelings of his four angry prospects. And that was the end of his sale, which he probably could have saved if he hadn't walked in at the worst possible moment.

Consequently, Dick Webster decided against going back for his fountain pen. Instead, he dropped the Robinsons a note, saying he would pick up his pen when he brought them the revised itineraries in a few days.